PENGUIN BOOKS
BBC BOOKS

WITH PASSPORT AND PARASOL

Julia Keay was born in Fife and now lives in Argyll with her husband, writer and broadcaster John Keay, and their four children. Her other works include *The Spy Who Never Was*, a biography of Mata Hari (Michael Joseph, 1987) and documentaries and plays for BBC radio. She and her husband are joint editors of the forthcoming *Collins Encyclopaedia of Scotland*.

JULIA KEAY

WITH PASSPORT AND PARASOL

THE ADVENTURES OF SEVEN
VICTORIAN LADIES

PENGUIN BOOKS
BBC BOOKS

PENGUIN BOOKS
BBC BOOKS

Published by the Penguin Group and BBC Enterprises Ltd
Penguin Books Ltd, 27 Wrights Lane, London W8 5TZ, England
Penguin Books USA Inc., 375 Hudson Street, New York, New York 10014, USA
Penguin Books Australia Ltd, Ringwood, Victoria, Australia
Penguin Books Canada Ltd, 10 Alcorn Avenue, Toronto, Ontario,
Canada M4V 3B2
Penguin Books (NZ) Ltd, 182–190 Wairau Road, Auckland 10, New Zealand

Penguin Books Ltd, Registered Offices: Harmondsworth, Middlesex, England

First published by BBC Books, a division of BBC Enterprises Ltd 1989
Published by Penguin Books and BBC Books, a division of BBC Enterprises Ltd 1994
1 3 5 7 9 10 8 6 4 2

Printed in England by Clays Ltd, St Ives plc

CONTENTS

ACKNOWLEDGEMENTS

I am grateful to the Estate of Alexandra David-Neel for permission to quote at length from *My Journey to Lhasa* and *Magic and Mystery in Tibet*, and to John Murray (Publishers) Ltd for permission to quote from *The Passing of the Aborigines* by Daisy Bates. Katharine Crerar and Barbie Crawford have been most helpful in supplying family details and recollections of their cousin, Gertrude Bell; and H.V. Winstone, Gertrude Bell's biographer, and Lesley Gordon, custodian of the Gertrude Bell papers in the University of Newcastle, have been generous with their expertise and advice. My thanks, too, to Helen Crerar for her researches at Abu Simbel, and to William Bristowe's daughter, Mrs Belinda Brocklehurst, for providing the wonderful photographs from her father's collection and for her kind encouragement. My husband, John, has been a tower of strength throughout.

The bibliography at the end of this book lists the main works I have consulted, but amongst them are several that deserve a more direct mention. For the most part these are full-length biographies or memoirs of the ladies whose lives I have only been able to sketch, and I owe a great debt of gratitude to their authors. These are in particular Janet Dunbar's *Golden Interlude, The Edens in India 1836–42*; William Bristowe's *Louis and the King of Siam*; H.V. Winstone's *Gertrude Bell*; Elizabeth Salter's *Daisy Bates, Great White Queen of the Never-Never* and Ernestine Hill's *Kabbarli, A Personal Memoir of Daisy Bates*.

This book is dedicated to the memory of Alan Haydock who, as long ago as 1984, wanted me to write it. In the event, his sad and untimely death in 1987 meant that not only did he not see it, but he never even knew it was to be written. I hope he would have approved.

PICTURE CREDITS

Cover

Fine Arts Photography.

Inside

Page i *main picture* portrait by F. Rochard 1935, from *Simla* by Pat Barr and Ray Desmond, Scolar Press 1978, *inset* from *Portraits of the People and Princes of India* by Emily Eden 1844; pages ii and iii *all* from the collection of the late Dr W. S. Bristowe; page iv *top* Hulton Picture Company, *bottom* from *A Thousand Miles up the Nile* by Amelia Edwards 1877; page v *top and bottom left* from *On Sledge and Horseback to Outcast Siberian Lepers* by Kate Marsden 1892, *bottom right* Mary Evans Picture Library; page vi *top left* Hulton Picture Company, *top right* University of Newcastle upon Tyne, *bottom* Royal Geographical Society; page vii *top* National Library of Australia, *bottom* Australian Overseas Information Service, London; page viii *top* from *My Journey to Lhasa* by Alexandra David-Neel 1927, *bottom* Fondation Alexandra David-Neel.

PROGRAMME CREDITS

With Passport and Parasol:
Seven True Stories of Travel and Adventure
compiled and written by Julia Keay

'An Unforgettable Vision' with
Dorothy Tutin as Alexandra David-Neel
Daniel Massey as the Narrator

'Notions of Liberty' with
Sian Phillips as Anna Leonowens
John Franklyn-Robbins as the
Narrator and Garard Green as the
King of Siam

'Baptised of the Desert' with
Rosalie Crutchley as Gertrude Bell
Paul Daneman as the Narrator

'Mere Mortals and Englishwomen'
with
Anna Massey as Amelia Edwards
Peter Marinker as the Narrator and
John Baddeley as 'Murray's Guide'

'Scarcely a Sacrifice'
with
Sinead Cusack as Daisy Bates
Edward de Souza as the Narrator

'Highly Respected Miss Kate'
with
Jill Balcon as Kate Marsden
Richard Bebb as the Narrator

'Never Send a Son to India, My Dear'
with
Sarah Badel as Emily Eden
Richard Pasco as the Narrator

The series was directed by John Powell and first broadcast on BBC Radio 4
in June and July 1988.

When the idea of writing a book to accompany the radio series *With Passport and Parasol* was first mooted, I hesitated. The seven ladies featured in the series had been selected from a short-list of about a dozen; the final choice falling on those who (a) had not previously been the subject of a radio documentary and (b) had written in sufficient volume about their own lives/philosophies/travels to satisfy the demands of the format. That they were, in the end, a disparate bunch and the links between them decidedly tenuous mattered less than that their stories made good radio.

A book, I thought, should surely be more cohesive. The main characters would somehow have to be drawn together into an identifiable group. It turned out to be like trying to round up a flock of chickens; I would catch three or four – and the rest would escape with indignant squawks and an explosion of feathers. Stay calm, let them settle, look again; they have to have some things in common.

Thanks to the extraordinary longevity of Queen Victoria they could all, at a pinch, be described as Victorians, although the lives of the earliest and the latest overlapped by only a year; certainly they were all female – but then so is more than half the world's population; they all made their names/fortunes/lives overseas, so they could be described as travellers – but that would be misleading. The label 'traveller' implies someone for whom travelling is an end in itself, and probably only for Amelia Edwards was that the case. For the others travelling was variously unavoidable, coincidental, a pleasurable bonus or an occupational hazard – but generally subordinate to their real interests.

Perhaps they were all escaping from the stifling restrictions imposed on women by contemporary European society. Gertrude Bell would speak of the feeling of exhilaration as she embarked on her first independent journey: 'the gates of the enclosed garden are thrown open, the chain at the entrance of the sanctuary is lowered . . . and behold, the immeasurable world.'

When Alexandra David-Neel was asked why she spent so much of her life in the back of beyond, she recalled an early craving 'to go beyond the garden gate, to follow the road that passed it by, and to set out for the unknown'. A link? Possibly. But it was immediately snapped by Emily Eden's thoughts from the threshold: 'for a person who required nothing but to be allowed the undisturbed enjoyment of my small . . . house and garden, I have been very hardly treated.'

The possibility that they all departed their native shores for the sake of their health led me off on another search. I did not get very far. True, Daisy Bates had an early tendency towards consumption, and Emily Eden was plagued by dreadful headaches as soon as she was bored. But Amelia Edwards prided herself on never having suffered a day's illness in her life; Gertrude Bell felt 'like the immortal Gods for health', but decided she probably slept better than they did; and Alexandra David-Neel attributed her astonishingly robust constitution to 'fresh air, long tramps' and a hot cup of tea at the start of every day. The *coup de grâce* was delivered to the theory by Kate Marsden and Anna Leonowens, both of whom suffered ill health as a result of their excursions rather than the other way round.

Even the fact that they were all female only led to more distinctions between them. The most striking of these was that while Amelia Edwards was a Vice-President of the Society for Promoting Women's Suffrage, Gertrude Bell was an active member of the Anti-Suffrage League. By the early nineteenth century European men were trotting round the globe in considerable numbers – but in many of its remoter corners, even a hundred years later, European women were still an unknown species. Each one of these seven must therefore have realised that her sex set her apart. Yet only three, Emily Eden, Daisy Bates and Anna Leonowens, seemed to feel any particular sympathy for or interest in the women they met along the way, and of these only Anna Leonowens was moved actively to promote their cause. Gertrude Bell dismissed other women as irrelevant. Alexandra David-Neel was interested in Tibetan women, as she was interested in Tibetan weather or the Tibetan landscape, only when they were exceptional. Kate Marsden's sympathy embraced all humanity regardless of sex, and Amelia Edwards, so sturdy in defence of her fellow Englishwomen, rarely got close enough to the 'natives' to be able to distinguish male from female.

From whichever angle I looked at them, the result was the same: one or other of the seven, and sometimes most of them, escaped the muster. Some were grand, some humble; some famous, some unknown; some respected, some reviled; some were single, some married (though none happily so) and one widowed. When I ran down the list of their occupations the task began to look hopeless. They include a journalist, a tourist, a society hostess, a teacher, a nurse, a scholar and one who can best be described as a seeker after truth. Their chosen fields, too, could hardly have been further flung – Australia, Egypt, Siberia India, Siam, the Middle East and Central Asia. Since none of them apparently felt herself to be in any way representative of her sex it was even denied me to present them as a comprehensive cross-section of womankind.

Where, then, the cohesion?

Fortunately it soon struck me that my efforts were not just exhausting and fruitless, they were also inappropriate. The seven ladies were, *par excellence*, individuals. They deserve, not to be lumped together like a flock of chickens or that old auction-room standard 'a dustbin and contents', but to be displayed as separate items in a gallery.

That realisation illuminated the whole project. With each one under her own spotlight, their diversity was revealed as a virtue rather than a disadvantage. There was no longer any need to try and find common ground between Emily Eden, society hostess turned First Lady of British India, and Anna Leonowens, wife turned widow of a clerk in the Indian Civil Service. Gertrude Bell, the historian and scholar who spoke five languages fluently and was competent in several more, no longer sat strangely in the company of Amelia Edwards, the tourist who had to turn to her phrase book to order her breakfast. Kate Marsden's eleven-month dash through the wilds of Russia does not pale into insignificance beside Daisy Bates's thirty-five year sojourn in the wilds of Australia. And if like could only associate with like, Alexandra David-Neel could never be included in any anthology – how many French lady lamas have there ever been?

CHAPTER ONE

'DUTY CALLS'
· *Emily Eden* ·

ntentionally itinerant Emily Eden was not. The last thing on her mind in the spring of 1835 was foreign travel – quite the reverse in fact. What she wanted more than anything else in the world was a home of her own. It need not be grand. A cottage would do: a cosy room with an armchair by the fire, shelves for her books, walls for her pictures and windowsills for her plants – and maybe a little patch of garden where, if the sun shone and her health held out, she could stroll with her dog, help prune the roses or tie in the straying wisteria. A little comfort and tranquillity for her declining years – surely not an impossible dream for a genteel spinster on the threshold of middle age.

Instead she was being forced to lead the life of a vagrant. Her possessions were all stored in packing cases, she never knew from one day to the next which case contained her clothes and, worst of all, she was running out of married sisters to stay with. She had certainly been made very welcome by all five of them in turn; but a maiden aunt must eventually become a burden, however well she was loved.

The blame for her predicament lay firmly at the door of the government. For the past year, as the political fortunes of the Whigs and Tories had see-sawed, her life had been in turmoil. It had been bad enough when Lord Melbourne had promoted her brother George, Lord Auckland, to the position of First Lord of the Admiralty. She had wept at being forced to leave their lovely house in Greenwich and move to the vast draughty apartment in Admiralty House.

Everybody says what fortunate people we are, and I daresay George *is*, but my personal luck consists of having lost Greenwich – the charm of my life – being kept in London – which I loathe – and being told to have people to dinner, without the means of dressing myself for society. I wish Government would consider that, though a man be raised high in office, yet that the unfortunate women remain just as poor as ever.

Then, in October 1834, had come a rumour that Lord Melbourne was planning to send George out to India as Governor-General. It had been the merest whisper in the wind, but enough to give Emily a dreadful fright. 'Mercifully', Emily had written to her dearest friend, Theresa Lister, 'the danger is past. I knew it was too bad to be true, although that is a dangerous assertion to make in most cases, as it only hastens the catastrophe. But this was such an extreme case, such a horrible supposition that there was nothing for it but to bully it away. To be sent to Botany Bay would be a joke by comparison. There is a decent climate to begin with, and the fun of a little felony first. But to be sent to Calcutta . . .!' In the light of her relief, the bleak rooms of Admiralty House had taken on a new and homely glow.

Six months later the Whig government had collapsed, Sir Robert Peel and his awful Tories had taken over and poor dear George was out of a job. Although that was naturally a disappointment, at least it meant they could now retire back to the country. But even as she voiced her pleasure at the prospect she knew it was not to be. George insisted that there was no point in settling down anywhere – the Tory government was floundering and could not last. Melbourne would inevitably return as Prime Minister; he, George, could expect another government post and they would be faced with yet another domestic upheaval. Better wait and see.

So here she was – homeless. In what she could only describe as an unfeeling outburst, George had pointed out that even if she ran out of sisters to stay with, the doors of half the stately homes of England were open to her. He did not seem to understand that to be a guest in even the stateliest of someone else's homes could not compare with the joys of being the owner of your own, even if it was only 'a tent under a hedge where my tired mind may rest'.

Fate, however, had not forgotten the temptation Emily had cast in its path. In April 1835 there was another change of government; Peel resigned, Lord Melbourne once again became Prime Minister and within two weeks of taking office he offered George a new post – as Governor-General of India. 'What is there to say, except God's will be done,' wrote Emily to Theresa. 'I look forward to the climate with dread and to the voyage with utter aversion.'

Of the fourteen children of William Eden, First Baron Auckland, Emily and George had always been the closest and most devoted. Neither had ever married and together with their youngest sister, Fanny, they had shared a home for fourteen years. Throughout her brother's political career, from his days as a backbench Member of Parliament, through his succession to the House of Lords on the death of their father and his years both as President of the Board of Trade and First Lord of the Admiralty, Emily had acted as George's companion and hostess.

The prospect of taking on the role of First Lady in Calcutta held no fears for her. The Eden family had long moved in the most select of social circles, they were related by blood or marriage to some of the most illustrious families in the land, were on first-name terms with the rest and even counted the Royal Family among their close acquaintances. Despite Emily's current disgust with politics she had also long been a political animal and enjoyed nothing better than a lively debate over the dinner table with George's cabinet colleagues. The real calamity was the prospect of being separated from her friends and her family. Everything she had ever heard or read about India led her to believe it was a social and cultural graveyard. Once interred there she would be beyond the reach of everything that made life worth living – the latest books, the newest plays, the most up-to-date fashions and, above all, the current gossip. 'Every day my heart grows more sore. You do not and cannot guess what it is like.'

But although they were sympathetic in the extreme and as miserable as she was at the prospect of parting, her many friends were not taken in. They knew the Emily behind all the complaints: the less she had to worry about the more disgruntled she became and, conversely, the weightier her problems the more serene would be her smile. Her appearance, too, was deceptive: small and slight with long dark hair and a pale complexion that hinted at delicate health. Behind the frail facade, however, her friends knew her to be capable and really quite tough; she was shrewd and sharp-tongued and, since she did not suffer fools gladly, timid souls quaked at her readiness to speak her mind. But she could also be warm, witty and perceptive and had a delightfully dry sense of humour. The very qualities that made her such a valued and entertaining friend would not only carry her through the ordeal but ensure that those who were left at home would receive a lively account of her tribulations.

The outward and return journeys would account for a whole year, and since George's appointment was a political one, his term as Governor-General would last for as long as the Whigs remained in office. Emily therefore knew she could be away for as much as six years; 'an immense gap', she wrote to her eldest sister, Eleanor, Countess of Buckinghamshire, 'and coming at the wrong time of life. I shall miss your childrens' youth, and ours will be utterly over. When we meet again I shall be quite an old lady.'

It was not until 1857, following the Indian Mutiny, that the British government took over direct rule of India. In 1835 it was still nominally the responsibility of the East India Company to administer the affairs of those territories which had placed themselves under British protection. Ultimate control over all but the Company's commercial interests, however, lay in the hands of the India Office Board of Control in Whitehall. Although in theory the Governor-General took his orders from the Board of Control, it just was not practicable for every decision to be referred back to London when eight months could elapse between the despatch of a query from Calcutta and the arrival of a response from London. Although a Council of Ministers had been set up in Calcutta to advise and assist the Governor-General, the government of British India therefore effectively lay in the hands of one man. It was an awesome responsibility, but Emily had no doubt at all that George was equal to the task.

★   ★   ★   ★

To give them time to prepare for a domestic and official upheaval of such magnitude, their departure was set for the end of September. Fanny, the only other unmarried Eden sister, was to go with them and William Osborne, son of another sister, Charlotte, had been appointed George's Military Secretary, so Emily would not be entirely deprived of relations. While George was being briefed about India, Emily's first priority was to have portraits painted of as many of her nephews, nieces and godchildren as could be completed in time. Then those of her belongings that she would not be taking to India had to be packed, repacked and stored; farewell presents had to be sent to all her friends; and of course a whole new and unfamiliar wardrobe had to be assembled.

> You cannot think what a whirl and entanglement buying and measuring and trying-on makes in your brain. Nightdresses with short sleeves, and net night-caps because muslin is too hot. Then such anomalies – quantities of flannel which I never wear at all in this cool climate, but which we are to wear at night there because the creatures who are pulling all night at the punkahs sometimes fall asleep. Then you wake from the extreme heat and call to them, then they wake and begin pulling away with such vigour that you catch your death with a sudden chill. What a life! However, it is no use thinking about it.

They set sail from Portsmouth aboard the *Jupiter* on 3 October 1835. In addition to Emily, George, Fanny and William, the party included their physician, Dr Drummond, six personal servants, a French cook, Emily's King Charles spaniel, Chance, and William's pack of six hunting greyhounds. Having claimed that she so loathed water that not for a thousand pounds a day would she contemplate spending five months at sea, Emily was surprised to find that the voyage was really quite enjoyable.

We have had a very smooth sea and I can read and draw and write, and as we are all perfectly well, there is not much to complain about. Who would have thought that in the middle of winter, when we ought to be shivering in a thick yellow fog, George and I should instead be established on a pile of cushions in the stern window of his cabin, he without his coat, waistcoat and shoes, learning Hindoostanee by the sweat of his brow, and I with only one petticoat and a thin dressing-gown on, a large fan in one hand and a pen in the other. I never could like a sea life, nor do I believe anyone does, but with all our grumbling about ours, we could not have been 19 weeks at sea with so few inconveniences.

Having touched land in Madeira, Rio de Janeiro and Cape Town, the *Jupiter* finally reached Calcutta on 2 March 1836, Emily's thirty-ninth birthday. The arrival of any ship from England was an event that brought curious crowds to the quayside. The arrival of a new Governor-General was an unparalleled spectacle; the streets of Calcutta seethed with a brighter, more vociferous multitude than Emily had ever imagined. George, wearing his full regalia, was shown into the first carriage while Emily and Fanny, suffocating in their best gowns, took their places in the second. What with the tightness of her collar, the heat of the sun and the crush of the crowd, Emily thought she must surely disgrace them all by fainting dead away, and her anxiety made the short ride to Government House seem endless. The only thing that kept her upright in the carriage was the thought of collapsing on a proper bed in a cool, quiet room with the blinds drawn. It was a little galling, therefore, to be informed on their arrival at the door that 'the eighty guests who had been invited to a "small" reception in our honour would be arriving hot on our heels. . . . Thus we start – and thus, I suppose, we shall continue'.

So bewildering was their new life that it was not until nearly the end of March that Emily got round to picking up her pen. 'We have been here three weeks today but I cannot help thinking that we have been here much longer and that it is nearly time to go home again. It is an odd, dreamy existence in many respects, but horribly fatiguing . . . it is like a constant theatrical presentation; everything is so picturesque and un-English.'

Her fears about the limitations of society and the lack of companionship were yet to be realised – first she had to get used to the grandeur.

I get up at eight, and with the assistance of three maids, contrive to have a bath and be dressed for breakfast at nine. When I leave my rooms I find my two tailors sitting cross-legged in the passage making my gowns, a sweeper plying his broom, two bearers pulling the punkahs and a sentry to mind that none of these steal anything. I am followed down the stairs by my Jemadar or head servant, four Hurkarus or couriers who are my particular attendants and by Chance, my spaniel, carried under his own servant's arm. At the bottom of the stairs I find two more bearers with a sedan chair in case I feel too exhausted to walk to the immense marble hall where we dine. All these people are dressed in white muslin with red and gold turbans and sashes, and are so picturesque that when I can find no other employment for them I make them sit for their pictures.

Emily's skill as an artist was one of the enduring joys of her life in India. The country and its people provided a profusion of irresistible subjects for her sketch-book, and she is remembered now almost as much for the high quality of her watercolours and line drawings as for the eloquence of her letters. But, as she hastened to assure her friends, for all the luxury, hers was far from an idle life. Since the departure of the previous Governor-General, Lord William Bentinck, the position had been filled by an acting Governor-General, Sir Charles Metcalfe – a bachelor. The arrival of Lord Auckland and his sisters meant that Calcutta society – such as it was – now had a hostess in Government House for the first time in two years. Indeed, not just one hostess but two. Emily and Fanny's timetable was almost as full as George's. On Mondays they had to preside over the Governor-General's official dinner party; on Wednesdays they were expected to be 'at home' to the select group of notables whose names graced what was called the 'Government House List' and on Tuesday and Thursday mornings they had to receive anyone else who chose to call, 'sometimes as many as 100 or 120 visiting in two hours'. Given this heavy social schedule it did not take Emily long to make up her expert mind about Calcutta society. It was even worse than she had anticipated.

Topics of interest we have none indigenous to the soil. There is a great deal of gossip, I believe, but in the first place I do not know the people sufficiently by name or by sight to attach the right history to the right face, even if I wanted to hear it, and we could not get into intimacies even if we wished it, for in our *despotic* government, where the whole patronage of this immense country is in the hands of the Governor-General, the intimacy of any one person here would put the rest of society into a fume, and it is too hot for any super-induced fuming. Indeed it is so very HOT I do not know how to spell it large enough.

As the summer advanced Emily found the horrors of Calcutta's 'polite society' quite eclipsed by the horrors of its climate. In November she was still complaining that although it was now 'what is by courtesy known as the "cold weather", yet I have not been able to live five minutes day or night without the punkah and we keep our blinds closed as long as there is a ray of sun'. She still complained, too, that there was not one pleasing or accomplished woman amongst her entire European acquaintance in India. But her attitude towards her fellow countrywomen – particularly the younger ones – was mellowing. She could hardly bear to look at the fresh, cheerful faces of new arrivals from England. The best that even the luckiest among them could hope for was to leave India in ten or twenty years time alive; many would be dead long before that as a result of disease or the climate; others would have to face the agony of burying their children, and even those who took the accepted precaution of sending their children home to school 'are more to be pitied than it is possible to say'.

Her own health seemed to be standing up tolerably well to the strain. 'Although I have been rather ailing for ten days, in general I have much better health here than I have at home,' she wrote on the first anniversary of their arrival. But by December 1837 she had changed her tune.

> Everybody who was here when we came has either gone home or up the country. We are a very limited group and have lost all semblance of cultivation. Indeed I am almost certain we are very nearly savages – not the least ferocious, not cannibals, not even mischievous – but simply good natured, unsophisticated savages, fond of finery, precious stones and tobacco, quite uninformed, very indolent and rather stupid. We are all dying of fevers brought on by the rainy season and the only topic of interest is our approaching journey. I have decided the only way I shall survive it is by embarking on an interminable course of sketching.

* * * *

The approaching journey had been planned by Lord Auckland in response to the one issue that would dominate his whole term in office – Afghanistan. The threat of an invasion of India from Russia by way of Central Asia had been hanging over successive Governors-General for more than thirty years. In the wake of Russia's recent success in its war with Persia, this threat had grown not only more real, but physically closer. The British government was convinced that the next step would be a Russian advance on the Afghan capital of Kabul – the obvious launching pad for an invasion of India.

These fears had recently been reinforced by rumours that the Afghans were looking for Russian assistance in a long-running territorial dispute with Ranjit Singh of the Punjab. Urgent steps must obviously be taken to pre-empt this dangerous alliance. So, after months of discussion and debate, both with the government at home and with his agents on the ground, Lord Auckland had decided to make a grand tour through the border states. The tour would culminate in a state visit to the court of Ranjit Singh, the most important of all these independent rulers. An effective solution to the Afghan problem would be very much easier to implement with the co-operation and assistance of the 'Lion of the Punjab'.

'I make no objection', wrote Emily, 'though I do say that for a person who required nothing but to be allowed the undisturbed enjoyment of my small Greenwich house and garden, with all its little Cockney pleasures and pursuits, I am being very hardly treated and rather overworked.'

She was at it again. But this time her grumbles fooled no one. So pleased was she at the prospect of leaving Calcutta that she could really not be bothered to dissimulate. Her only excursions out of the city in twenty months had been weekend trips to Barrackpore, the Governor-General's official country house. The journey 'up the country' would be long, probably tedious and certainly extremely uncomfortable, but if it gave her a change of scene and a break from the relentless heat and humidity that had drained her of all energy and baked her 'a delicate shade of yellow', then it was a prospect to be welcomed.

The grand tour was an undertaking of mammoth proportions. George anticipated that it would last for eighteen months, but warned his sisters to be flexible in their expectations – it was impossible to estimate how long they might have to spend in careful negotiations with Ranjit Singh before any agreement could be reached. There would be frequent stops along the way as they entertained and were entertained in return by the Princes and Rajahs through whose territory they passed; and since it would be impossible to travel at all through the hottest months, they planned to make a prolonged stopover in Simla during the summer. The speed of their progress would also be dictated by the size of the official entourage. The Governor-General's household and staff of more than 500 people made up only a small fraction of the whole. An 8000-strong regiment would provide an escort, there would be military and political advisers, ADCs, doctors, clerks and clergymen, together with their families and their servants. There would be porters, cooks, tailors and messengers. There would be camel-herds, mahouts and grooms to look after the 850 camels, 160 elephants and thousands of horses, and there would be hundreds of tons of provisions and supplies. In all more than 12000 people would leave Calcutta for the 2000-mile journey – an impressive cavalcade, even by the elaborate standards of British India.

The main body of this mighty throng left Calcutta in advance and travelled overland to Benares. George, Emily and Fanny were to make this first stage of the journey by boat up the River Ganges; not until they assembled in Benares would the march proper begin. They left on 21 October 1837.

For the three and a half weeks that it took them to complete the 700 miles to Benares, the weather was so sultry and the scenery so monotonous that Emily began to wonder whether the tour was in fact going to be much of an improvement on staying put in Calcutta. When, upon reaching

Benares, she set eyes for the first time on the tents that would from now on be their home, her heart sank. 'We landed at five and drove four miles through immense crowds and much dust to our camp. The first evening of tents was more uncomfortable than I ever fancied. Everybody kept saying "What a magnificent camp." I thought I had never seen such squalid, melancholy discomfort.'

Ironically, in view of the amount of time they were to spend in each other's company, Emily and Fanny were the least close of the Eden sisters. They were fond enough of each other, but their interests and attitudes were poles apart. Fanny was only six years the younger but the difference could have been twice as great. Light-hearted and vivacious, she was thoroughly enjoying India and seemed to find the heat positively invigorating. She had made several 'up country' excursions from Calcutta with William and his friends and was therefore an old hand at what Emily disgustedly called 'this camping life'. Their respective attitudes to their tents neatly illustrated their respective attitudes to life in general; while Emily christened hers 'Misery Hall' and George's 'Foully Palace', Fanny called hers the 'Fairy Castle' and vowed she could happily live in it for the rest of her life.

Emily's 'melancholy squalor' consisted of four private tents for the Governor-General's party; one each for himself, Emily and Fanny with a fourth drawing-room tent making up the square. 'Misery Hall', 'Foully Palace' and the 'Fairy Castle' were each divided up into bedroom, dressing room and sitting room, all draped with embroidered wall-hangings and connected to each other by covered passages. Next to the Governor-General's enclosure were a vast dining tent for official dinner parties and an even larger durbar tent where George would host balls and receptions. Beyond these in every direction stretched the rest of the camp, tents arranged in lines to form streets – kitchen tents, stable tents, hospital tents and living quarters for the horde. But even though she would admit that it was an impressive sight, Emily never grew to like it. 'It feels open-airish and unsafe', she wrote, 'and I am, and always will remain, much pre-possessed in favour of houses.'

Each day this small town had to be dismantled and re-erected. Emily, Fanny and George soon grew accustomed to having their camp furniture whisked away from under them at the end of every evening in order that it could be packed up and ready for an early departure the next morning. But camp furniture did not mean deck chairs, fold-away tables and paper plates. After all, the Governor-General was showing the flag. Dinners were elaborate meals eaten at proper dining tables off the best Government House china; thick carpets covered the earthen floors, even the scenery, props and costumes of an entire theatre had been crated up and brought along in order that their guests might not find their entertainment lacking in any way. Once the entire column was on the move it stretched for ten miles and very often those at the head arrived at the next camp before those at the tail had left the previous one.

Although she grumbled at having to wake up each morning at five-thirty and be on the move by six, Emily was glad of the rule that stated no one could leave ahead of the Governor-General.

> We escape all the dust that way. We travel half the way on elephant and the other half on horseback. It is very pleasant and cool at that time of day, really nice weather, and we sometimes march for as little as seven or eight miles. It seems somehow wicked to move 12 000 people with their tents, elephants, camels, horses, trunks etc. for so little, but there is no help for it.

As the vast cavalcade lumbered slowly westward Emily found her thoughts dwelling less and less on her own discomforts. Government House in Calcutta had been very much an ivory tower in which she and Fanny, and to a lesser extent George too, had lived at several removes from the great mass of the Indian people. Now, for the first time, she was seeing India properly. She was seeing real people, smelling real smells, travelling through real landscape – without the barrier of a private compound and heavily-guarded wrought-iron railing to obscure her view. Certainly not everything she saw was pleasant and where her sensibilities or her nose or her artist's eye were offended she did not hesitate to say so: 'The moral of my Indian experience is that it is the most picturesque population with the ugliest scenery that was ever put together,' was her verdict after a month on the road. But she was refreshingly free of the hypocrisy and prejudice that would so heavily infect later generations of Anglo-Indians. 'I wish you would have one little brown baby for a change,' she wrote to one of her relentlessly prolific sisters, 'they are so much prettier than white children.'

She still longed to be in England, and the highlights of their progress were those days on which the 'dak', or postal runners, caught up with the camp. News of the preparations in London for the coronation of the young Queen Victoria put her in a rage for a week – it was so exactly the sort of occasion she adored and to miss all the excitement was almost more than she could bear. But there were compensations. Like the time they were invited to call on a particularly wealthy Rajah near Allahabad. His own elephants were sent to carry them to his palace. When they drew near in the dusk, they could see that not just the palace but the whole village had been decorated by millions of bright little oil lamps lining every doorway, every arch and every window ledge. Emily was impressed.

It was the largest illumination I ever saw. We went on the elephants through the great gateway, in a Timur the Tartar fashion, into the courtyard. Such torches and spearmen and drums and crowds, like a melodrama magnified by a microscope. We dismounted at the door of an immense court, and the Rajah's servants spread a path of scarlet and gold brocade for us to walk on. Considering that it costs a pound a yard and I had just decided I could not afford to buy enough of it to make a dressing-gown, it seemed a pity to trample on it.

The trials that she had to endure paled into insignificance when compared with those suffered by the British residents of some of the more remote up-country stations. How they survived what she called their 'horrible solitude' was beyond her comprehension. Even in Bengal and the other British protectorates, where the military and administrative personnel and their families usually formed a large enough group to qualify as an 'expatriate community', the loneliness and isolation of their lives were awful to contemplate.

Word of the approach of the Governor-General's mighty column had these 'poor forgotten creatures' in a fever of anticipation; the presence in their district of none other than Lord Auckland and his illustrious sisters, not to mention an entourage that consisted of more of their compatriots than they had seen in one place for years, seemed like a gift from heaven. It provided them with a unique opportunity to indulge in such forgotten pleasures as dressing up, dancing, listening to real music and, if their brains had not been addled by solitude, civilised conversation.

The significance of their presence was brought home to Emily by the fact that some of their guests were prepared to travel in great discomfort for as much as three days just to attend an official luncheon. The delight with which they greeted this desperately needed contact with their own kind gave Emily a real sense of purpose and of worth. If it was George's job to reinforce good relations with the native rulers of the autonomous states through which they passed, then it was hers and Fanny's to do what they could to alleviate the miseries of the British. For their sakes she would put up with the endless round of parties, balls and receptions; she would admire their gowns, share their nostalgia for such British delights as cold weather and cricket and listen to their problems with as much interest as she could muster, 'even though a great many of them have lived in the jungle for years and their manners are utterly gone – jungled out of them. Luckily the band plays loudly all through dinner and drowns most of the conversation.'

Her heart went out most of all to the young single men, mostly planters, traders and civilian employees of the East India Company, who had to live and work outside British territory. Of all imaginable ordeals, theirs was surely the worst. 'How some of these young men must detest their lives.

We met one last week who we had known in Calcutta and he was quite mad with delight at seeing us. He said the horror of being three months without seeing a European or hearing an English word no one can tell.' She had listened aghast as he had described how, towards the end of the rainy season when health and spirits are at their lowest ebb, he had been convinced that he was going to die and that if he did, there would be no one to bury him. Even more poignant had been the meeting with the stepson of 'Mrs O.', an acquaintance of hers in London, 'the one whose picture she used to carry about with her because he was such a beautiful creature'. This Adonis was now 'a bald-headed, grey, toothless old man and perfectly ignorant on all points but that of tiger hunting'. 'Never send a son to India, my dear', she warned Eleanor, 'that is the moral. And please to remember that I shall return from India a worn-out woman.'

✳   ✳   ✳   ✳

For the first two months of their march Emily was, in fact, very far from worn-out. The pity she felt for her compatriots overshadowed her habitual self-pity to such an extent that she was even prepared to admit that she was enjoying herself. Whenever she had a quiet moment out would come her sketch-book, and soon she had assembled a substantial portfolio of pencil-drawings and watercolours of people, temples, statues and landscapes. She even felt brave enough to make the occasional solitary expedition to sketch some particularly eye-catching scene.

Her pleasure was not destined to last. As 1837 turned into 1838, the cumbersome cavalcade passed through the kingdom of Oudh. The King's welcome was as lavish as any they had yet encountered, and his palaces as exquisite as any they had seen. But where Emily's eyes had been opened by the kaleidoscopic colour of India and then dazzled by the opulence with which it entertained her, now they wept at her first sight of the misery that lurked behind the magnificence. They left Cawnpore to find the tragedy of India sprawling at their feet.

> It is here that we came into the starving districts. They have had no rain for a year and a half, the cattle have all died and the people are all dying or gone away. The distress is perfectly dreadful, you cannot conceive the horrible sights we see, particularly children; perfect skeletons in many cases, their bones through the skin, without a rag of clothing and utterly unlike human beings. The sight is too shocking; the women look as if they had been buried, their skulls look so dreadful. I am sure there is no sort of violent atrocity I should not commit for food, with a starving baby. I should not stop to think about the rights or wrongs of the case.

It was typical of Emily that she did not turn her back on this tragedy. But she had been brought up in a strict tradition of *noblesse oblige*; where many of her contemporaries would have passed by on the other side, perfumed handkerchief pressed to haughty nose, she saw it as her duty to do what she could to help.

> When I went round to the stables yesterday before breakfast I found such a miserable little baby, something like an old monkey, but with glazed stupid eyes. I am sure you would have sobbed to see the way in which the little atom flew at a cup of milk. We have discovered the mother since, but she is a skeleton too and says that she has had no food to give it for a month. Dr Drummond says it cannot live it is so diseased with starvation but I mean to try what can be done with it.

Thanks to Emily's efforts the baby survived. But more than 800 000 people would die in the famine. Although the quartermasters in charge of the official stores handed out what they could in the way of relief supplies to the starving, the presence of the extra 12 000 people in the Governor-General's train could only exacerbate matters. For two weeks they pressed on at full speed to remove themselves from the famine area. Festivities were forgotten, there were no diverting sketching trips and little time for relaxation; the dust became more pervasive, the state of the roads deteriorated and the heat, which had relented for a while, returned with a vengeance. By the time they reached Delhi at the end of February, Emily was exhausted.

★   ★   ★   ★

Exposure to feast and famine, grotesque poverty and equally grotesque wealth might well have driven her to disgust with India, with all its contradictions and frustrations and inadequacies. But although she would continue to inveigh against the climate and the geography, and most of all against the very fact of being there rather than in her beloved England, Emily was developing a very real sympathy for the country and its people. In the early days her instinctive reaction to the strangeness of everything Indian had been a slightly mocking incredulity. The descriptions and anecdotes which had enlivened her letters and so vastly entertained their recipients had tended to caricature. But this was all changing. The more she learned, the greater became her respect for the people of this vast land. And the more she appreciated the anomalous position of the British in India the more they, rather than the Indians, became the target for her disapproval. While she could sympathise with the plight of the individual, she was very ready to criticise the excesses of the group. 'I am not very fond of Englishmen out of their own country,' she wrote from Delhi. 'Delhi is a very suggestive and moralising place – such stupendous remains of power and wealth passed and passing away, and somehow I feel that we horrid English have "gone and done it" . . . revenued it and spoiled it all.'

Once they left Delhi they were at last travelling north towards the hills. But the six weeks it took them to reach Simla were the most depressing so far. 'Our marching troubles increase every day,' Emily complained. 'The roads are so infernally bad – I beg your pardon but there is no other word for them – and I am so tired I can no longer sit on a horse.' Worst of all, though, was the fact that dear George seemed to be in such low spirits.

In fact 'dear George' was almost beside himself with worry and frustration. His agents in Afghanistan were sending increasingly pessimistic reports about the situation there. Their attempts to woo Dost Mohammed into an alliance had foundered; the town of Herat in western Afghanistan was under siege from a Persian army encouraged, partly financed and probably officered by Russians. Russian spies were reported to be everywhere and Lord Auckland knew that time was running out. Unless he moved quickly, Herat could fall, the Russian approach to India via Kandahar would be clear, and the dreaded invasion could be under way. So complete was Emily's faith in her brother's ability that although she herself never really understood what was going on in Afghanistan it never occurred to her that he was not totally in command of the situation. Instead she put his preoccupation down to the rigours of the journey.

They reached the foothills of the Himalayas in the middle of March. From now on their progress would be made even slower by the steep winding hill roads, but the sight of the mountains and the prospect of some cooler weather restored Emily's spirits considerably. She was even able to undergo the alarming experience of being whisked up 'perpendicular precipices' in a *jonpaun*, or open sedan chair, with no more than a gentle request to her bearers not to race each other round the corners.

At last, on 3 April, they reached Simla. Emily was in ecstasies.

Well it really is worth all the trouble – such a beautiful place – and such a climate! No wonder I could not live down below. We were never allowed a scrap of air to breathe – now I come back to the air again I remember all about it. It is a cool sort of stuff, refreshing, sweet and pleasant to the lungs. Our house only wants all the good furniture and carpets we have brought to be quite perfection. We have fires in every room, and the windows open; red rhododendron trees in bloom in every direction and beautiful walks like English shrubberies on all sides. . . . I see this to be the best part of India. Not that I would not set off this instant and go at top speed over all the hot plains and through the hot wind if I were told I might sail home the instant I arrived at Calcutta; but as no one makes me that offer I can wait here better than anywhere else – like meat, we keep better here.

Although it would be another twenty years before this sprightly little hill town became the official summer capital of the British Raj, already there was a sizeable British community in residence, on the run from the heat of the plains and trying to pretend they were not in India at all. The Governor-General's party would remain here for as long as it took to set up the state visit to Ranjit Singh in the Punjab. It was only her loyalty to George that stopped Emily from hoping that the arrangements would never be made.

As the hot season advanced the hill-station filled up – military men on leave, sportsmen on hunting trips and families with eager marriageable daughters – all in holiday mood. Every day seemed to bring some new form of entertainment. There were dinner parties and whist drives, amateur theatricals and rustic picnics, fêtes and horse races, weddings and dances. The stifling humidity of Calcutta and the grinding slog of life on the march seemed a long way off indeed. 'If the Himalayas were only a continuation of Primrose Hill or Penge Common I should have no objection to pass the rest of my life in them.'

Emily's new-found vitality took her servants quite by surprise – they did not know the *Burra Memsahib* could be so domesticated. She supervised her tailors as they stitched new chintz curtains for her drawing room, she taught her cook to make strawberry icecream and she filled several sketch-books with landscapes and portraits.

Yet her appreciation and enjoyment of all these English pleasures was tempered by an acute awareness of the absurdity of the whole situation. 'There we were', she commented after a day spent at a 'Fancy Fair', '105 Europeans surrounded by at least three thousand mountain men, wrapped up in their hill blankets, looking on at what we call our polite amusements and bowing to the ground if a European comes near them. I sometimes wonder they do not cut all our heads off and say no more about it.' Between activities she was content to potter about the garden of the Governor-General's Residence (renamed Auckland House in George's honour), super-vising the planting of shrubs and the establishment of an asparagus bed, or just sitting admiring the spectacular view, glorying in the cool weather and listening to 'English blackbirds' singing in the trees.

*   *   *   *

George, however, was having a less cheerful time. He was a man of many fine qualities; in private he was gentle and considerate, in his official dealings he had a reputation for being conscientious, meticulous and fair-minded. But he had one fault that would lead history to condemn him as 'the most inept of all Governors-General'; he was dangerously – and, in the case of Afghanistan, fatally – indecisive. The problems there had existed long before he had left Calcutta. Yet by the time he reached Simla he was still prevaricating. In fairness he was not helped by the political and personal animosity that existed between his two chief advisers, Colonel Wade in the Punjab and Captain Burnes in Kabul. Where Burnes was advocating concessions to and ultimate agreement with Dost Mohammed, Wade was pressing him to depose Dost Mohammed, who in view of his intransigence was obviously an unsuitable ally, and replace him with a more amenable monarch. Indeed he had just such a man in mind – Shah Shuja Mirza, the son of a previous king of Afghanistan who had himself been deposed by Dost Mohammed.

Burnes' plan to come to an agreement with Dost Mohammed would inevitably antagonise Ranjit Singh, a potentially valuable ally. Wade's plan to depose him and install Shah Shuja on the throne in his place, on the other hand, could only be achieved by force of arms. Lord Auckland quite simply could not decide which was the lesser of the two evils. It was only when William McNaghten, his Political Secretary, came down firmly on the side of Wade that he finally – and catastrophically – made up his mind. Dost Mohammed must go.

> 'All these tendencies towards war are rather nervous work', wrote Emily in August. 'Poor George, he feels his responsibility so, no Ministers, no Parliament, and his Council, such as it is, down in Calcutta; he has a great deal to answer for by himself, but I daresay he does it very well.'

So much confidence did she have in George's wisdom that, although she shuddered at the thought of all that bloodshed, Emily concentrated firmly on the silver lining. 'We gain one good by this war. It is not thought suitable for George to meet Ranjit Singh until he can escort him at the head of 10000 men and the army cannot muster until the end of November. So that gives us three more cool weeks here and takes off three very hot weeks of the plains'. But a new dimension was added to negotiations with the Sikh leader, for George intended to persuade him to contribute both funds and troops to the plan to depose Dost Mohammed. To this end he sent a deputation to the Maharajah's court in the Punjab and invited a reciprocal delegation to visit him in Simla. Their arrival created quite a stir and Emily rose majestically to the occasion – only to find that her efforts were less than fully appreciated.

> We have had a Sikh deputation here for nearly a week. They dress quite beautifully and speak the most flowery nonsense you can imagine about roses blooming in the garden of friendship and nightingales singing in the bowers of affection since the two powers have approached each other. We have been

entertaining them in grand style and I try to help George by conversing politely with them, but they do not like much talk from a woman. The poor ignorant creatures are perfectly unconscious what a very superior article an English-woman is. They think us contemptible if anything, which is a mistake.

The Sikh delegates were under strict instructions from their master. Ranjit Singh was entirely in favour of removing his old foe from the throne of Afghanistan. He had no intention of using either his own men or his own money to achieve this coup, but to have said so outright would have been to jeopardise a plan that suited him very well. The 'flowery nonsense' was designed to flatter and to deceive, and it succeeded in both. When the final arrangements were made for the great meeting, George was still happily under the illusion that the desired assistance would be forthcoming.

★   ★   ★   ★

This day fortnight we are to be in our wretched tents – I could have a fit of hysterics when I think of it. The work of packing progresses and there are no bounds to the ardour with which everybody labours to make us uncomfortable. Already there are horrible signs of preparation with camel trunks and stores going off. A great many people have to go down to the plains this week. Poor things, it is about as rational as if a slice of bread were to get off the plate and put itself on the toasting fork.

The idyll was over. On 9 November 1838, after seven delicious months in Simla, they 'returned to the tramping way of life'. This time there was none of the excitement that had attended their departure from Calcutta, none of the relief at leaving the heat and humidity that had raised Emily's spirits and reconciled her to some degree to the discomforts of life on the move, none of the novelty of seeing new people and places that had been some compensation for the lack of amiable company. Simla had allowed her to unpack and dust off all her dreams of England; she had been able to reconstruct something of their image among the tulips and the rhododen-dron bushes and the cool fresh air. Now even that fragile edifice was being torn down – England was once again slipping beyond her grasp. Although George had been playing down the gravity of the Afghan situation in order to spare his sisters' anxiety, they could not help being aware of the sombre atmosphere amongst his officials. An elusive but ominous shadow seemed to lurk in their midst and darken their departure, and Emily's desperation was compounded by the weather.

We have been six days in camp and it is pouring as it only pours in India. It is impossible to describe the squalid misery; little ditches run round or through each tent with a slosh of mud that one invariably steps into; the servants look soaked and wretched, the camels slip down and die in every direction; I have to go under an umbrella to George's tent and we are carried in palanquins to the dining tent. How people who might by economy and taking in washing and plain work have a comfortable back attic in the neighbourhood of Manchester Square, with a fireplace and a boarded floor, can come and march about India, I cannot guess.

It had been arranged that the great meeting between the Governor-General of India and the Lion of the Punjab would take place at Ferozepore on the border between British India and the Punjab. Ranjit Singh had already set up his camp on the western bank of the Sutlej river; the British Army of the Indus, 14 000-strong and poised to accompany the pretender to the Afghan throne into Kabul, was already stationed on the eastern bank. On 26 November, Lord Auckland and his party arrived to complete the scene.

Instead of the neat, almost civilised little tented town that had sprung up at every halt on their way up-country from Calcutta, the camp on the Sutlej seemed to Emily to resemble Bedlam. 'The cavalry are pitched just behind our tents,' she complained, 'one horse gets loose and goes and bites all the others, and then they kick and get loose too and all the syces wake up and begin screaming and tent pitchers are called in to knock in the rope pins and the horses all neigh till they are tied up again. Then the regiment has got a mad drummer (or two or three) who begins drumming at five in the morning and never intermits until seven. I suppose it is some military manoeuvre, but I wish he would not.'

The climate, the noise and air of tension in the camp were threatening to demolish the few remaining strands of her patience and her temper. She had been suffering from recurring headaches ever since leaving Simla. She had travelled the whole way to Ferozepore in a carriage with blinds drawn, refusing to eat, unwilling to speak to anyone and quite unable to write letters; and the moment they reached the Sutlej she retired to her bed.

But curiosity was a powerful restorative. As soon as order had been established in the camp, George was to entertain Ranjit Singh to the first of the whole series of durbars, receptions, parades, breakfast parties and fêtes that had been planned to celebrate their historic meeting. It would have taken more than a headache to keep Emily from her first sight of the notorious Maharajah. Within hours of their first encounter she was scurrying for her pen, all aches forgotten.

Today was the great day. George and all the gentlemen went on their elephants to meet Ranjit who arrived on an equal number of elephants – indeed there were so many that the clash at meeting was very destructive to howdahs and hangings. George handed the Maharajah into the large tent where he sat down for a few minutes on the sofa between George and me.

Emily was fascinated. Here was the man who, from obscure origins, had built himself an empire stretching from Tibet to Afghanistan and down the Indus to the deserts of Rajasthan and Sind; the military genius whose courage was legendary and whose political insight had impressed even the most arrogant of British officials; the absolute ruler of a most unruly people and the finest horseman in the Sikh army. 'I certainly should not guess any part of this from looking at him,' she wrote. 'He is exactly like an old mouse, with grey whiskers and one eye.' He was very small, almost a dwarf, and even his good eye was failing. His face was pockmarked, his speech slurred and his bearing ungainly. Yet somehow she was not disappointed. Even though he was adorned in nothing more glamorous than 'the commonest red silk dress and no jewels whatever', this 'funny old man' seemed every inch the great king. His solitary eye blazed with animation, his hands were alive with expression and he exuded an extraordinary energy.

Delicacy prevented her from mentioning the other half of Ranjit Singh's reputation – that of a sensual degenerate whose excesses had profoundly shocked many a sturdy British emissary to his court. But it was most certainly known to her and added more than a little spice to her fascination.

Before any serious business could be discussed between the principals, there were essential rituals to observe. First the various regiments of the Army of the Indus had to parade before the Maharajah, colours flying and bands playing. Then it was Ranjit's turn to show George something of the strength and magnificence of his own forces. Perched uncomfortably on a podium under the shade of a gold-embroidered awning, Emily and Fanny were suitably impressed. The pageant outshone any spectacle they had ever attended, and even went some way towards compensating them for having missed Queen Victoria's coronation. Whole troops of Sikh cavalry galloped and wheeled before them, the men dressed in red or yellow satin, the horses trapped out in gold and silver; hundreds of elephants, decorated all over with ornate painted patterns and glittering jewels; fifty of Ranjit's favourite horses from the royal stud with cruppers of emeralds, stud-ropes of gold, necklaces of huge pearls and saddle-cloths encrusted with diamonds. Even the ever-loyal Emily had to admit that the spectacle 'reduces European magnificence to a very low pitch'.

For three weeks it seemed that the only object on either side was to outshine the other. Great trays of gifts crossed the Sutlej river between the two camps; the finest cashmere shawls for Emily and Fanny, a portrait of Queen Victoria copied by Emily from prints sent out from England and framed in solid gold for Ranjit Singh, a gold bed encrusted with rubies and draped in yellow silk for George, an elephant and six horses with gold trappings for the Maharajah, and jewels of startling size and inestimable value for everyone. It was one of Emily's favourite grumbles that East India Company policy forbade anyone, even the Governor-General or his sisters, to keep even the smallest and least valuable official gift, but she now admitted to suffering from 'a surfeit of diamonds'. The rivalry extended to entertainments too. When Ranjit hosted a dinner in the centre of a flower garden that had been brought, posy by fragrant posy, all the way from Lahore for the occasion, George responded with a fête for which the British compound was laid out in a similar fashion, but with forty-two thousand little oil lamps instead of flowers.

As the First Lady, Emily was invariably seated at the Maharajah's right hand at these elaborate parties, an honour that gave her a chance to observe the little man more closely. As soon as he sat down an attendant presented the Maharajah with a gold bottle of his favourite tipple – a fiery liquid so potent that lesser men had been known to pass out after a single glass. On one occasion he insisted that Emily taste it which, for fear of offending him, she tried to do. 'A single drop actually burnt my lips – I could not possibly swallow it.' One of George's ADCs, when challenged by Ranjit to a drinking bout, survived only by contriving to empty several glasses on the carpet under the table, an expedient adopted by Emily herself with the stream of delicacies that the Maharajah insisted on passing to her off his own plate in his none-too-clean fingers. Less genteel observers of his conduct than Miss Eden reported that he would even leave his seat, pee in the corner of the tent and return quite unconcernedly to the feast. Certainly his behaviour was so extraordinary and unpredictable that Emily sometimes found the entire meal had passed without her having eaten a mouthful. More than once she could have sworn he was winking at her, though it was hard to distinguish a wink from a blink when he had only one eye, and although she only suspected him of trying to flirt with her it was very obvious that he took great delight in trying to shock her. Miss Eden took equal delight in refusing to be shocked. It would take more than 'a drunken old profligate' like the Maharajah to upset the composure of the Governor-General's sister.

* * * *

Once the niceties were out of the way politics took over. The negotiations dragged on, with Lord Auckland now totally committed to Wade's plan and the Maharajah equally determined not to become directly involved. In the middle of December Ranjit Singh fell ill – 'hardly surprising in view of his excesses', thought Emily – and the whole camp moved with him back to Lahore. As her third Christmas in India came and went Emily felt a great weariness sweep over her. She was too tired to take in the details of the treaty that was finally signed between the two powers, and oblivious of the crafty way in which Ranjit had managed to pass on the responsibility for supporting the Army of the Indus to the Amirs of Sind. If George thought he could succeed in installing Shah Shuja on the throne in Kabul without the help of the Maharajah, then she was sure he was right.

The ill-fated Army was finally despatched towards Afghanistan early in the New Year of 1839. It would take some months to reach Kabul and while its future was uncertain there was no possibility of the Governor-General returning to Calcutta. So, after a long detour via Delhi, Emily found herself back in Simla for a second summer. The news that trickled through from Afghanistan was better than they could have hoped. In April Kandahar fell and by August the British Army, with Shah Shuja at its head and McNaghten and Burnes at his side, had finally entered Kabul. After fierce fighting Dost Mohammed was put to flight and the British puppet was installed on the throne. The news reached Simla hard on the heels of the news of the death of Ranjit Singh in Lahore. Emily's sadness at the passing of her old sparring partner was tempered by her pride when word came from London that George was to be made an earl in recognition of his great achievement in Afghanistan.

The first indication that all might not be well came in December as the Governor-General and his entourage reached Agra on their way back to Calcutta. Dost Mohammed was reported to be massing an army of his own and threatening Kabul. The population of Kabul, whom British despatches had initially described as welcoming Shah Shuja with open arms, was now admitted to be openly hostile to his ineffectual rule. Instead of being able to withdraw and leave Shah Shuja in control, the Army of the Indus now appeared to be in need of reinforcements. 'An awful change has taken place in our plans – one that makes me sick to think of,' wrote Emily from Agra on Christmas Eve. 'There is so much to watch over in Afghanistan that George has decided he cannot leave for Calcutta. We are to stay here for the next ten months. I am in such a mood about it that I should almost be glad if the Sikhs, or Russians, or anybody, would come and take us all. It would be one way out of the country.'

Only a week into the New Year she was writing again, 'Well, there never were such times! I am too old for these quick changes, but I am glad of this one. George woke me this morning by poking his head into the tent and saying "Here is the overland mail come, and all my plans are changed, and we are going straight to Calcutta." I am so happy I could do like the native servants. They are all quite mad, flinging themselves on the ground, and throwing off their turbans and thanking their Lordship for taking them back to their families.'

The overland mail had brought news of another international incident that looked likely to turn into war. The Chinese authorities had closed the port of Canton to all trade in opium, striking a crippling blow to one of the East India Company's most valuable exports. It was George's responsibility as Governor-General of India, and thus the East India Company's most senior official in the region, to see that the trade was not interrupted. So urgently was his presence required, in fact, that he would have to leave immediately and travel directly and independently to Calcutta. 'George's going is a great grief,' wailed Emily. 'It is impossible to live without him here.' But really she was just jealous that he would be escaping the crawling misery of the camp and arriving at journey's end so far ahead of her.

Not until the end of February 1840 could Emily and Fanny finally bid farewell to the tents that had been their home on and off for two and a half years. Reaching Allahabad Emily made a vow: 'That is positively the last time in my natural life in which I will make a long dusty journey before breakfast.' As she surveyed the remnants of the camp she realised that they had only just made it in time. Everything appeared to be in shreds, even the patches on the tents had holes in them, the furniture was falling to bits, the china was all cracked, and as for her own wardrobe, well 'the right shoe of my only remaining pair has sprung a large hole, my last gown is torn to fringes and my last bonnet is brown with dust.' As she trailed the dusty fringes of her last gown up the steps of Government House in Calcutta on 1 March, Emily reflected that it was almost as good as arriving home.

However her dream of leaving India for good in March 1841 was not to be realised. The election in England that was to have marked the end of George's term was postponed and he was ordered to stay on. There seemed no end to the nightmare. But far worse was to come. Reports from Afghanistan now spoke of rebellion and intrigue, of British officers being stoned in the streets of Kabul and powerful tribes gathering in revolt against Shah Shuja and the Army of occupation. Lord Auckland received instructions from London to withdraw the Army of the Indus in the face of both this hostility and the colossal expenditure involved in keeping it in place. Now he made his second fatal mistake. Instead of obeying these instructions he preferred to listen to the advice, once again, of McNaghten in Kabul who could still not believe that Dost Mohammed was strong enough to return. By the end of the year both Burnes and McNaghten had been murdered, their bodies hacked to pieces and paraded before a cheering crowd, and the remnants of the glorious Army of the Indus was in ignominious retreat. Of more than 5000 men who fled Kabul in January 1842, only a handful survived the slaughter.

Emily could do nothing except sit and watch George grow old before her eyes. To the extent that the advice he had taken had been McNaghten's, she argued that the blame for the monumental tragedy should also lie with McNaghten. But she knew – as did George – that that was not how things worked. The ultimate responsibility lay with the Governor-General. Despite the many and considerable achievements of his six years in office, Lord Auckland would be remembered as the man responsible for a defeat of the British Army in Asia second only in magnitude to the loss of Singapore.

In the postponed election in London, which had finally taken place in July 1841, the Whigs had been defeated and the Tories were now back in power. The new Governor-General, Lord Ellenborough, arrived in Calcutta in the spring of 1842. As soon as he was safely installed George, Emily and Fanny were free to leave India at last. The moment Emily had been looking forward to for six long years had finally arrived – and all she could do was weep.

*   *   *   *

After their return to England Emily, George and Fanny set up home together in Kensington, in a villa on the site of what is now the Royal Geographical Society. Despite her permanent preoccupation with her own health, Emily, in the end, would outlive both her elder brother and her younger sister by twenty years. George died suddenly on New Year's Day 1849 of a cerebral haemorrhage and Fanny, at the age of only forty-eight, died four months later of heart failure. Emily was desolate.

For the rest of her life her great consolations would be the company of her many nephews and nieces, her correspondence with her friends, and her writing. Her first novel, *The Semi-Detached House*, was published in 1859 and her second, *The Semi-Detached Couple*, in 1860. Though these would both enjoy considerable critical acclaim, the most popular and successful of her books would be the selection of her own letters from India, published in 1866 under the title *Up the Country*.

She died in August 1869 at the age of seventy-two.

'NOTIONS OF LIBERTY'
· Anna Leonowens ·

n January 1862, His Excellency the Siamese Consul in Singapore requested an interview with the proprietress of a small school for the children of British officers. At the subsequent meeting he explained his purpose; His Majesty Somdetch P'hra Paramendr Maha Mongkut, the Supreme King of Siam, was looking for an English governess to undertake the education of his children and he had been instructed to enquire whether the honourable lady would be prepared to entertain the project.

The proprietress's name was Anna Leonowens. And her instinctive reaction was to say no – she knew nothing about Siam, its people or its king; she had no friends or even aquaintances there, and she could not speak a word of the language. But once the Consul had taken his leave she found herself reflecting on the suggestion and on her current circumstances. She was thirty-one years old, a widow, the mother of two small children and, thanks to the annoying habit so prevalent among British officers of forgetting to pay their childrens' fees, her school was not thriving. The longer she reflected, the more feasible and even attractive the Consul's offer appeared.

Finally, on the reasonable assumption that the Supreme King of Siam might prove a more reliable employer, she contacted the Consul and informed him that she was after all willing to 'entertain the project'. A month later a letter arrived at the school:

Grand Royal Palace, Bangkok. Madam, we are in good pleasure and satisfaction in heart that you are in willingness to undertake the education of our beloved royal children. And we hope that in doing your education on us and on our children (whom English call inhabitants of benighted land) you will do your best endeavour for knowledge of English language, science and literature, and not for conversion to Christianity; as the followers of Buddha are mostly aware of the powerfulness of truth and virtue as well as the followers of Christ, and are desirous to have facility of English language more than new religions. Believe me, Yours faithfully S.P.P. Maha Mongkut.

Within three weeks of receiving this picturesque communication Anna Leonowens left Singapore for Bangkok.

★   ★   ★   ★

The 1950s musical *The King and I*, which was based on Anna's experiences in Siam, would portray Mongkut as a cross between Attila the Hun and Coco the Clown. As Anna would discover, there were elements of both the despot and the buffoon in the man who was about to become her employer, but these were just two small fragments in a very elaborate mosaic. She herself would be portrayed as a patronising American widow who wore crinolines eight feet across, who taught the King to waltz, and who spent most of her time surrounded by adoring little princesses, gazing at a willow-pattern landscape and singing mournful songs about the tribulations of young love – less offensive, perhaps, but not much more accurate.

The visionaries of the theatrical world were responsible for many of the distortions, but some of the blame must also lie at Anna's door. When she came to write about her years as *The English Governess at the Siamese Court*, she would dramatise, exaggerate and even fabricate parts of her story in order to attract the general reader to what she thought would otherwise be a book for the specialist. The inaccuracies were then compounded by her biographer who, understandably, took Anna's version at face value and then subjected it to her own interpretation. By the time the story of *Anna and the King of Siam* was set to music it had therefore been processed by three separate and vivid imaginations – so it is hardly surprising that it bore only a passing resemblance to the truth.

Anna's own version of her childhood, and the one on which her biography was based, states that she was born in Caernarvon in 1834, that her father was Captain (later Colonel) Thomas Maxwell Crawford of the Indian Army and that her parents returned to India when Anna was six years old, leaving Anna and her sister in the care of an aunt in Wales.

At the age of sixteen, we learn, the gently-nurtured Anna went out to join her parents in India where she shortly met and fell in love with Lieutenant (later Major) Thomas Leonowens of the Commissariat Department of the Army. They were married in 1851 and moved to a comfortable and colourful house on the outskirts of Bombay. Their first two children died in infancy and the young couple moved to London for the sake of Anna's health. While they were in London two more children were born to them, a daughter Avis in 1854 and a son Louis in 1855.

The following year Thomas was ordered to rejoin his regiment in Singapore; in the summer of 1857 the Agra Bank in India collapsed during the Indian Mutiny – and Anna's comfortable inheritance from her late parents went with it. Then in 1858, we learn, came the worst disaster of all – Thomas died of heatstroke after riding home from a regimental tiger-shoot through the heat of the day. Anna was now a poverty-stricken widow. In order to support her children she started up her school in Singapore, and it was in this capacity that she came to the notice of the Siamese emissary.

All perfectly plausible, and it was not until the 1970s that anyone thought to query her story. When historian William Bristowe started to research the life of Anna's son Louis, however, he discovered a very different Anna. In his book *Louis and the King of Siam* Mr Bristowe reveals that her father was a Sergeant Edwards, not a Captain Crawford, she was born in Ahmednagar, not Caernarvon, her husband was plain Mr Thomas Leon Owens, a clerk in the Military Pay Office, and he died from apoplexy while running a hotel in Penang, not from heatstroke while returning from a tiger-shoot. Although their first two children did die in infancy and the third and fourth, Avis and Louis, survived, the rest of the story was fictional. The lost fortune in Agra never existed, the sheltered childhood in Wales was a much more rough-and-ready upbringing in Bombay, although it did apparently include a spell at school in England, and, horror of horrors, the distressed gentlewoman may even have had 'a touch of the tar-brush in her veins'. The invention dated from the death of her husband. Anna was twenty-eight years old, her parents were both dead and she had no wish to return to her remaining relations in India.

Because they have been so much better documented, the lives led by army officers and their families are taken to be representative of the lives of all the British in India. Not so. For the 'other ranks', life in India was often a grim affair that had very little to do with elegant drawing rooms, turbanned servants and idle self-indulgence. Crowded into that uncomfortable and insalubrious no-man's land that divided officers and gentlemen on one side from the native Indians on the other, they found themselves either spurned or completely ignored by both. It was to escape from this ghetto that Anna and Thomas eventually left India six years after their marriage. They arrived in Penang with their two children in 1856.

Very little is known about Thomas Leon Owens – and Anna herself mentioned him only rarely and obliquely in her books – but it seems that he was ambitious and that he made a moderate success of running the hotel in Penang. Although a hotel-keeper was only a step or two above a clerk on the social ladder, at least he was free from the paralysing bureaucracy of the lower echelons of the Indian Civil Service, and by the time he died only two years later he had saved enough money to ensure that Anna and their two children were not left destitute. But his death was a cruel blow. While he had been by her side she had given hardly a thought to the security of her foothold; now she suddenly realised that halfway up a ladder was no place to be on your own. To have slithered back down to her origins would have been a betrayal of her and Thomas's dreams. The only alternative was to scramble as quickly as possible for the top.

In addition to a bravely independent spirit Anna had a great deal of determination and, surprisingly, a flair for languages; her otherwise undistinguished education in England had included French lessons, she and Thomas had studied both Hindustani and Sanskrit in Bombay, and she had quickly learned to speak Malay in Penang. These qualifications gave her an idea – not just how she and her children might survive, but perhaps how she might be able to pick up her parasol and glide out of no-man's land into polite society. But she knew that if her new venture was to succeed she would need more than a little money and a talented tongue – she would need credentials.

There were three things she had to do; she had to move away from Penang where too many people knew her, she had to invent for herself a new past, and she had to learn – fast.

The move to Singapore had been quite straightforward, and Thomas's money was sufficient to allow her to start up the school. The matter of her background had been easy too – she had promoted her father from Sergeant to Colonel, her husband from Mister to Major, and hinted at an inherited fortune lost during the upheavals of the Indian Mutiny, all of which had helped persuade the officers that she was a suitable person to whom to entrust the education of their children. The learning, however, had proved a little more tricky.

The nuances of 'the Queen's English' were easy enough to master, although Anna sometimes got carried away by her own eloquence, but the finer points of ladylike conduct were harder to pin down. Perhaps because she was unfamiliar with the real thing, she took as her model of 'a lady' the romanticised ideal of Victorian womanhood. Her account of the various situations she met with in Siam, and of her own actions and reactions to them, is irresistibly reminiscent of the paintings and prints of the time: drama piles upon melodrama, dashing heroes and black-hearted villains chase each other across the pages while innocent, curly-headed children, faithful pets and fragile, misty-eyed mothers endure all manner of ordeals with a brave, long-suffering smile. Because this picture was superimposed on someone who was very far from the Victorian ideal – someone who had probably only ever been misty-eyed when she was chopping onions and whose instinctive reaction to being called fragile might well have been to throw a plate at whoever made the suggestion – the results were not entirely convincing. They were sufficient to qualify her to teach the children of polite society – but somehow polite society had not opened its doors to her. The move to Siam, particularly since it also involved stepping into royal circles, seemed to offer her just as much respectability, far more security and a chance to escape from the beady eyes of Singapore society.

In fact Anna was doing herself a great disservice by adopting the mannerisms and attitudes she ascribed to 'the quality'. Not many of her social peers were as observant, as articulate or as adventurous as she was, and if she had only written a straightforward account of her experiences, her recollections would have been unique. The very things that she was now battling not just to escape but to disguise – her modest background and the fact that she was forced to earn her own living – would have earned her the admiration and respect of readers, historians and armchair travellers alike. She would have been a startling and very welcome exception to the vast majority of her contemporary travellers who were, to quote Dorothy Middleton, 'middle-aged, middle-class and in poor health'.

Sadly, but understandably, she chose rather to try and emulate them, and while it is easy to sympathise with the loneliness and insecurity that led her to dissemble, it is hard not to mourn the lost opportunity. It would be intriguing, for example, to know what she really thought of Bangkok. She had never been to Siam, and the interval between her acceptance of the Consul's offer and her departure had been so short she had not had time to learn much about her future home. Her first sight of the city would therefore naturally have given rise to some feelings of apprehension. But to one who had spent most of her life in the East, it would have surely been no more terrifying than the first sight of Marseilles or Venice would have been to a Londoner. Writing years later for readers who might find the travel-weary shrug of a veteran a strange response from one whom they believed to be an innocent abroad, she chose rather to describe it from the wide-eyed viewpoint of a novice.

> As night approached the gloom and mystery of the pagan land into which we were penetrating filled me with an indefinable dread. Here was a strange floating city, with its stranger people on all the open porches, quays and jetties; the innumerable rafts and boats, canoes and gondolas, junks and ships; the pall of black smoke from the steamer, the burly roar of the engine, the bewildering cries of men, women and children, the shouting of dockworkers and the barking of dogs – yet no one seemed troubled but me.

But she was not inventing the tears that filled her eyes when her small son clung to her for comfort on the deck of the *Chao Phraya*. At six years old

Louis had been considered too young to leave his mother. Together with his *ayah*, Beebe, the *ayah*'s husband Munshee, and a Newfoundland dog called Bessy, Louis would stay with Anna for the duration of her stay in Bangkok. However Anna had arranged before leaving Singapore for eight-year-old Avis to be sent back to school in England, and she knew she would not see her daughter again for some years. 'The memory of her tender farewell blinded my outlook and as, with a rude jerk, we came to anchor, so with a shock and a tremor I came to my hard realities.'

Within minutes of the *Chao Phraya* dropping anchor, the river was alive with small boats 'worked by amphibious creatures, half naked, who rent the air with shrill wild jargon as they scrambled towards us'. Suddenly, as if by magic, a clear channel opened through the thronging, bobbing mass of boats and a showy gondola, shaped like a dragon and lit by blazing torches, drew alongside the steamer. From this exotic craft a Siamese official mounted the side 'with an absolute air'. Anna, the real Anna this time, was more startled by the reaction of the crew of the *Chao Phraya* than by this apparition, for every 'Asiatic' aboard, with the exception of Beebe and Munshee, immediately crumpled to his knees and pressed his forehead to the deck. Not until the apparition gave the appropriate sign of consent did the captain of the steamer make the introductions. 'His Excellency Chow Phra Suriyawongse, Prime Minister of the Kingdom of Siam.'

To be welcomed by the Prime Minister in person was most gratifying. Even though he was 'half-naked and without an emblem to denote his rank', there was something remarkable about Suriyawongse that held the eye and compelled respect. Anna – uncharacteristically – submitted quietly to his appraisal. Then, 'with an air of command oddly at variance with his almost indecent attire, of which he seemed superbly unconscious, he beckoned to an interpreter who, at a word, began to question me in English.'

Her gratification soon turned to dismay. As soon as the Prime Minister had ascertained that she was indeed the expected governess he turned to leave. When she asked him what plans had been made for her accommodation he replied abruptly that he had no idea, that the King could not be expected to remember everything and that she could go where she pleased. He then climbed down into his boat and was paddled back to the quay.

If the over-elaborate language and the wide-eyed innocence are dead giveaways, so too is Anna's response to authority. Like a convert to Catholicism – or any other -ism for that matter – she was far quicker to take offence at any supposed slight to her adopted status than anyone who had been born to it. Subordination, like chopping onions, was something she had left behind her; ladies of quality surely did not have to defer to anyone, even Prime Ministers or Kings. Instead of meeting what she called this 'heartless, arbitrary insolence on the part of my employers' with dignity, she burst into tears of rage and mortification.

In the event Anna and Louis were rescued by the timely arrival of Captain Bush, the English harbourmaster, who invited them to spend the night at his home. Anna's composure was much restored by Mrs Bush's solicitous welcome, and she responded quite graciously when a 'slave' appeared the following morning to take them to the Prime Minister's palace.

> The interpreter led us through a suite of spacious rooms, all carpeted, cande-labraed and appointed in the most costly European fashion. A superb vase of silver, embossed and burnished, stood on a table inlaid with mother-of-pearl and chased with silver. Flowers of great variety and beauty filled the rooms with a delicious fragrance. On every side my eyes were delighted with rare vases, jewelled cups and boxes, dainty statuettes – *objects de virtu*, Oriental and European, antique and modern, blending the old barbaric splendors with the graces of the younger arts.

When she suddenly found herself face to face with Suriyawongse, 'the semi-nude barbarian of last night', her hackles prepared to rise. Fortunately the Prime Minister unintentionally defused the situation by holding out his hand and saying 'Good morning, sir,' which comical form of address momentarily punctured her haughty pose. His kindly smile for Louis and courteous enquiries after her health encouraged her to raise the matter of her accommodation, and, politely but firmly, she outlined her requirements – a quiet house or apartments where she might be free from intrusion and at perfect liberty before and after school hours. The Prime Minister's reaction was ominous. 'He stood looking at me, smiling, as if surprised that I should have notions on the subject of liberty.'

Suriyawongse was indeed puzzled. He simply could not understand why a lady with no husband should feel the need for either liberty or privacy. But when he proceeded to question her motives for making such a strange request she leapt back onto her high horse. Why she wanted private apartments and what she intended to do in them was none of his business – would he kindly not pry into her domestic concerns. Had the Prime Minister been less restrained Anna might have learned a valuable lesson here, for when he reacted to this defiance by turning on his heel and marching out of the room, she thought for an awful moment that she might have been too bold. As it was, when one of his attendants appeared and signed to her to follow him, her doubts vanished. Obviously she had got it just right.

The servant led them to the far end of the palace and showed them into a suite of charming rooms opening onto a small terrace shaded by blossoming fruit trees and overlooking a small artificial lake. But Anna had little time to appreciate their comforts, for no sooner had she removed her shawl than the doors burst open to admit 'with a pell-mell rush and screams of laughter', a gaggle of excited young ladies – Suriyawongse's harem.

Since she was neither a typically prim Victorian nor a narrow-minded, bigoted Christian, Anna was not shocked by the harem itself. Harems were a fact of oriental life with which she had been familiar since childhood, and it simply did not occur to her to be embarrassed by this evidence of what her model would surely have called 'moral degeneracy' on the part of the Prime Minister. Neither would she throw up her hands in horror at the discovery that the King had over a hundred wives and concubines, and that thirty-five of these ladies would provide him, in the end, with eighty-two children. But what she did find horrifying was the life these ladies were condemned to live. A life, to her, of unimaginable confinement, constant surveillance and abject dependence. Although the education of the royal children was to be her official task, the plight of the royal concubines would be her greatest concern for the next five years, and she would tread on many sensitive toes in the course of her crusade on their behalf.

So, although she was longing for some peace to settle into her new quarters, she restricted her complaints at the intrusion to the observation that 'to be free to make a stunning din is a Siamese woman's idea of perfect enjoyment', and submitted to their boisterous curiosity without complaint.

*   *   *   *

It is easy to understand why the Siamese people took such exception to the portrait of their sovereign in *The King and I*. Although Yul Brynner's characterisation was very entertaining, it was wildly inaccurate. Far from striding energetically about his palace whistling, or taking waltzing lessons from his children's governess, the real Mongkut was frail, abstemious, partially paralysed as a result of a stroke, and had spent twenty-seven years as a Buddhist monk before succeeding to the throne in 1851. A crime almost greater than the misrepresentation, however, was the very fact that he had been portrayed at all: this amounted not only to *lese-majesty* but very nearly to sacrilege, for Mongkut was regarded – as had been his ancestors and as are his successors to this day – not merely as royal, but as divine.

History has proclaimed Somdetch P'hra Paramendr Maha Mongkut as 'one of the great Asians of the nineteenth century' and 'the man who managed to preserve his country's independence when, by the end of the nineteenth century, every other state in South-East Asia had come under European control'. A prodigious scholar, he had delved deeply into history, geography, physics, chemistry, mathematics, archaeology and astronomy and had spent many years studying the ancient Buddhist texts and teachings. In addition to English he spoke Laotian, Cambodian, Vietnamese, Burmese, Malay and Hindustani, and his mastery of Sanskrit and Pali, the classical languages of Buddhism, was unequalled even among the top academics in the land.

His studies and training in the monastery had also given him a much clearer understanding both of the needs of his people and of international affairs than any of his predecessors had possessed. On succeeding to the throne he had immediately set in motion a number of radical reforms in the laws, customs and institutions of his country that earned him respect and admiration both at home and abroad. When Anna arrived in Siam this remarkable monarch was fifty-seven years old, but she knew little about him beyond the fact that the mere mention of his name was enough to send a frisson – of excitement? Apprehension? She could not be sure which – through the assembled company.

When the day came for her to be presented to His Supreme Majesty, her nervousness made her prickly and defensive. It had been agreed that Captain Bush would make the introductions. 'Behold me', she would later exhort her readers, 'just after sunset on a pleasant day in April 1862, on the threshold of the outer court of the Grand Palace, accompanied by my own brave little boy, and escorted by a compatriot.'

> A flood of light sweeping through the spacious Hall of Audience displayed a throng of noblemen in waiting. None turned a glance, or seemingly a thought, on us, and, my child being tired and hungry, I urged Captain Bush to present us without delay. At once we mounted the marble steps and entered the brilliant hall unannounced. Ranged on the carpet were many prostrate, mute and motionless forms, over whose heads to step was a temptation as drolly natural as it was dangerous. His Majesty spied us quickly and advanced, petulantly screaming 'Who? Who? Who?'

Although officials, commoners and slaves alike were expected to prostrate themselves before any member of the Siamese royal family (a practice that Anna found outrageous), Mongkut knew better than to expect foreigners to follow the same rule. When Captain Bush introduced her as the English governess the King therefore quite amiably shook her by the hand. Out of the corner of her eye she could see a ripple of shock pass through the recumbent company at this unprecedented gesture – a reaction that gave her a perverse satisfaction and prompted her to a deplorable *faux pas*. The King asked her how old she was; 'scarcely able to repress a smile at a proceeding so absurd, and with my sex's distaste for so serious a question, I demurely replied "One hundred and fifty years old".'

She was supremely unconscious of how dangerous it was even to be suspected of making a mockery of His Majesty, and just as unaware that she had breached not just his social code but that of her imaginary model. But, as she had misinterpreted Suriyawongse's reaction to her demands, now she misinterpreted Mongkut's reaction to her discourtesy. For the King's manners were far better than her own; instead of taking offence and instantly dismissing her from his presence or indeed from his employ, he chose to accept her reply as a jest.

He also decided to cut short this public and unpredictable interview and beckoned her to follow him out of the Audience Hall. With a startled Louis clinging desperately to her skirt, Anna found herself being led along a maze of corridors to meet the youngest of Mongkut's many wives, a special favourite who would be among her pupils. As he limped on ahead of her, Mongkut outlined in the colourful English of which he was so proud the extent of her duties.

> I have sixty-seven children. You shall educate them, and as many of my wives, likewise, as may wish to learn English. And I have much correspondence with which you must assist me. And, moreover, I have much difficulty for reading and translating French letters; for the French are fond of using gloomily deceiving terms. You must undertake; and you shall make all their murky sentences and gloomily deceiving propositions clear to me. And, furthermore, I have by every mail foreign letters whose writing is not easily read by me. You shall copy on round hand for my readily perusal thereof.

Rather to Anna's relief it transpired that the royal astrologers had not yet fixed on a propitious day for the commencement of her classes. For the moment she was free to concentrate on learning Siamese, the better to communicate with her pupils when the moment should arrive. But she was still determined to procure suitable accommodation for herself and Louis, and for Beebe and Munshee, somewhere away from the claustrophobic noise and bustle of the palace. And as the Prime Minister had shown no signs of finding her such a haven, she decided to raise the matter with the King himself. However Mongkut, like Suriyawongse, was unable to understand why she should object to living within the palace; their second interview was no less fraught than the first.

> I told him that, being as yet unable to speak the language, and the gates being shut every evening, I should feel like an unhappy prisoner in the palace. I reminded him that in his letter he had promised me a residence adjoining the palace, not within it. He turned and looked at me, his face growing almost purple with rage. He shouted that he did not know what he had promised, all he knew was that I was his servant, that it was his pleasure that I stay in the palace and that I MUST OBEY HIM. These last words he fairly screamed. I trembled in every limb and for some time knew not how to reply. At length I ventured to

say 'I am prepared to obey all your Majesty's commands within the obligation of my duty to your family, but beyond that I can promise no obedience.'

Louis burst into tears and the women who had witnessed the angry interchange gasped in horror. With a low bow to his outraged Majesty, Anna withdrew to her apartments. She was no longer a servant and she *would not* be treated like one.

Mongkut's unusual patience with his recalcitrant new employee must have stemmed from the knowledge that English governesses were something of a rarity in South-East Asia, and that Anna had been highly recommended for her skills as a teacher. But if he could not send her away, he could at least teach her a lesson. A few days after their explosive encounter, a message arrived with the news that the King was reconciled to the idea of her living outside the palace, that a house had been selected for her, and a messenger waited to conduct her to it.

Vastly relieved, Anna fetched a shawl, called to Louis and accompanied the messenger down to the river. A slender boat took them a short way upstream and then pulled in to a pier. Alighting from the boat they were then led along a succession of ever smaller alleys, past a congestion of ramshackle warehouses, down 'a most execrable lane' and finally up three broken brick steps to a small dark door. The messenger produced a key and opened the door for Anna to step inside. She found herself looking into two filthy, windowless rooms stinking of putrid fish and containing a three-legged table, two broken chairs and a heap of mouldy mattresses.

> Rebuked and saddened, I abandoned my long-cherished hope of a home, and resigned myself with no good grace to my routine of study and instruction. Where were all the romantic fancies and proud anticipations with which I had accepted the position of governess to the royal family of Siam? Alas, in two squalid rooms at the end of a Bangkok fish market.

To make sure the lesson had been fully learned Mongkut did not contact Anna for two months. But finally he relented, or as Anna would have it, 'His Golden Footed Majesty presently repented him of his arbitrary cantankerousness' and another messenger arrived to take her on a second expedition. Set in a small 'piazza' sheltered by trees and looking over the river towards the royal palace, this house had nine rooms, most of them pleasantly airy, and 'every modern convenience, though somewhat oriental as to style of bath, kitchen etc'. Since it had obviously been empty for some time it was extremely dirty. But Anna was more than satisfied. As soon as the messenger had left she took off her hat and cloak, slipped on an old wrapper and set to with soap and water. Behind the closed doors of her own home she was quite happy to shed her airs and pick up a scrubbing brush.

★   ★   ★   ★

They were to enjoy just one night of glorious independence before the summons came from the King. The astrologers had pronounced – school was to begin. After the weeks of frustration and confusion, it was a relief to Anna to be able to get down to work. Every morning a boat would collect her and Louis from their house and take them across the river to the palace for lessons. The classroom was an ornate, marble-floored, gold-pillared pavilion with a high, vaulted roof and her pupils sat on gilded chairs at highly polished tables surrounded by vases of lotus blossoms – a far cry from the echoing floor-boards and ink-stained desks of her school in Singapore. The twenty-one 'scions of Siamese royalty' ranged in age from the Princess Ying You Wahlacks who was in her early twenties to a chubby little prince who could not have been more than three or four years old, and included the ten-year-old Crown Prince Chulalongkorn, 'a handsome lad, neither noticeably tall or short'.

Although Chulalongkorn was not the eldest of Mongkut's sons, he was the eldest son of the Queen Consort, and therefore held first rank among the children of the King as the heir-apparent to the throne. Anna found him to be 'modest and affectionate, serene and gentle, and an assiduous student'. In fact she was impressed not only with the charm, obedience and self-possession of her royal pupils, but also with the general level of education throughout Siam. Thanks to the diligence of the Buddhist monks, and the fact that every monastery was equipped with a library, the literacy rate, even among the poorer classes, was extraordinarily high. 'Thus most of my pupils were familiar with the process of education and very willing to learn.'

Had she been prepared to work strictly within the terms of her employment, Anna's relationship with the King would have prospered. She was an excellent teacher and he was more than satisfied with the progress his children made under her instruction. He greatly appreciated, too, her services as interpreter and secretary – an appreciation that, as the months passed, was increasingly reciprocated. For despite his unpredictability, Anna was beginning to understand that Mongkut was a man of many virtues.

Of Somdetch P'hra Paramendr Maha Mongkut it may safely be said (for all his capriciousness of temper and his snappish greed of power) that he was the most remarkable of the Oriental princes of the present century. Considered apart from his domestic relations, he was in many respects an able and virtuous ruler. His foreign policy was liberal, he extended toleration to all religious sects, he expended a generous portion of his revenues in public improvements and did much to improve the conditions of his subjects. And, most diligently of all, he was a progressive and enlightened scholar, more systematically educated, and a more capacious devourer of books and news, than perhaps any man of equal rank in our day. In many grave considerations he displayed soundness of understanding, clearness of judgement and a genuine nobility of mind, established upon universal ethics and philosophic reasons.

While she was generous enough to acknowledge his virtues, Anna never forgave Mongkut for destroying her illusions. The aberrations of his 'domestic relations' proved to her that even royalty – surely the epitome of respectability – could have feet of clay. She thought him 'envious, revengeful and subtle – as fickle and petulant as he was suspicious and cruel'; he had a ferocious and unpredictable temper, he bullied his wives, terrorised his servants and trusted no one; indeed the only saving grace of this 'forlorn despot' was the obvious love he had for his children.

There were two other barriers, in Anna's eyes, that stood in the way of Mongkut's 'advance in the direction of true greatness', and it was her confrontation of these barriers – which were really none of her business – that would disrupt their potentially comfortable relationship. The first was that although he was an ardent reformer he still condoned slavery, and did not share Anna's own horror at the way not only his slaves, but every one of his officials, was required to grovel on the ground at his approach.

Twice a week at sunset he appeared at one of the gates of the palace to hear the complaints and petitions of the poorest of his subjects who at no other time or place could reach his ear. It was most pitiful to see the helpless, awestricken wretches, prostrate and abject as toads, many too terrified to present the precious petition after all.

The second barrier concerned the ladies of the King's harem. As well as giving English lessons to those of his wives and concubines who wished to learn, Anna was allowed free access to the women's quarters and was always assured of a warm welcome from the inmates. They plied her with questions about herself, her husband and her children, they tried on her hat and cloak, paraded round their secluded garden draped in her veils amid shrieks of laughter, and would listen for hours at a time to her stories of the outside world. Anna played with their children, practised her conversational Siamese and listened in return to the stories of their lives.

Mongkut's wives and concubines were a cosmopolitan collection. Most of them were of gentle blood, 'the fairest of the daughters of Siamese noblemen and of princes of the adjacent tributary states', but there were also Chinese, Indians, Cambodians, Laotians and Malays. Some were presented as gifts to the King from officials wishing to gain royal favour, others were purchased specially for the harem by Mongkut's agents throughout South-

East Asia. Anna was startled to discover that enormous sums were being offered by these agents for 'an English woman of beauty and good parentage to crown the sensational collection'. But by the time she left Bangkok the coveted specimen had not yet appeared in the market.

It seemed quite extraordinary to the self-reliant Anna that many of these ladies appeared not merely resigned to their fate but actually quite happy with it. Having fought so hard to gain and maintain her own independence she could not understand how these, her 'ill-fated sisters imprisoned without a crime', could submit so meekly to such subjugation. Her indignation roused her to new heights of eloquence.

> I had never beheld misery till I found it here; I had never looked upon the sickening hideousness of slavery till I encountered its features here; pain, darkness, death and eternal emptiness, a darkness to which there is neither beginning nor end, a living which is neither of this world or the next. The misery which checks the pulse and thrills the heart with pity in one's common walks about the city is hardly so saddening as the nameless, mocking wretchedness of these women, to whom poverty were a luxury and houselessness as a draught of pure, free air.

It must be said, too, that it was something of a novelty for her to find herself the object of so much respect and admiration. When word reached the harem of her defiance in the face of what she called 'the King's more outrageous caprices', its inmates adopted her as their champion. The giggled titbits of gossip were now interspersed with grievances whispered shyly in her ear in the hope that she would plead their various causes with His Majesty. 'And so, with no intention on my part, I suffered myself to be set up between the oppressor and the oppressed.'

It is quite possible that, had Anna been more tactful in her approach, both the ladies of the harem and the royal slaves would have benefited from her espousal of their cause. But she made the mistake of imagining that she and she alone was aware of the injustices that undoubtedly existed both in the court and in the country as a whole. Since she had very little idea of the conditions that had prevailed in Siam before Mongkut came to the throne, she was in no position to appreciate how many reforms he had already put in hand. The abolition of slavery was high on Mongkut's list of reforms yet to be carried out; and Anna's assumption that he was unaware of the need for such a reform filled him with righteous indignation.

> Mem Leonowens, the governess of the royal children, is becoming very naughty. She meddles in His Majesty's affairs and has shown herself to be very audacious. She is more careful about what is right and what is wrong than about obedience and submission. Let her know that when princes and noblemen are

dissuaded from offering their daughters to the king as concubines, the king will cease to receive contributions of women in that capacity.

Instead the eventual implementation of these reforms may even have been postponed by this clash, for Mongkut had no intention of letting Anna think it was her influence that prompted them. Having expressed his displeasure first in a furious outburst and then by ignoring her completely for several weeks, he finally decided that her meddling had been a result of her not having enough to do. Anna found herself having to work far into the night to keep up with his ever-increasing demands; 'what with teaching, translating, copying, dictating, reading, I had hardly a moment I could call my own.'

In the end it took a tragedy to heal the breach between the King and the governess. One of Anna's most endearing pupils was the eight-year-old Princess Fa-ying. The only daughter of Mongkut's best-loved and most senior wife, who had died soon after the child was born, Princess Fa-ying held a very special place in the King's affections. When she professed a dislike for her Sanskrit teacher, Mongkut gave her permission to spend the time learning to draw and paint with Anna instead. Perhaps reminded by the child of her own daughter Avis, Anna grew very fond of Fa-ying. 'Never did work seem more like pleasure than it did to me as I sat with this bright little princess, day after day, at the hour when all her brothers and sisters were at their Sanskrit.'

One morning in the spring of 1864, when Anna and Louis were sitting on their piazza watching the bustle of boats on the river, a royal barge swept across from the palace towards them. A slave jumped out and handed Anna a letter.

My dear Mam, our well-loved daughter, your favourite pupil, is attacked with cholera and has earnest desire to see you and is heard much to make frequent repetition of your name. I beg that you will favour her wish. I fear her illness is mortal as there has been three deaths this morning. She is best beloved of my children. I am your afflicted friend, S.P.P. Maha Mongkut.

Horrified, Anna leapt into the royal barge and ordered the rowers to take her directly and at full speed to the palace. She was escorted at a run to the princess's quarters, pushed her way through the knots of anxious attendants thronging the corridors and arrived, panting, at Fa-ying's bedside.

Too late. Even the doctor had come too late. As I stooped to imprint a parting kiss on the little face that had been so fair, her kindred and slaves exchanged their prayers for a sudden burst of heart-rending cries. An attendant hurried me to the king who, reading the heavy tidings in my silence, covered his face with his hands and wept passionately.

The mercurial Mongkut was as quick to praise as he was to blame. Not many days later the same royal barge that had summoned her to the child's deathbed arrived at her house with another summons. When they reached the palace they were conducted this time to the school pavilion which had been decorated for the occasion with great banks of flowers. Anna was invited to sit in her 'chair of office' which had been painted bright red and festooned with garlands. When she had taken her seat somewhat reluctantly on the still tacky paint, a group of slaves entered carrying the late princess's schoolbooks which they stacked round Anna's feet and covered with fresh roses and lilies. The doors at the end of the pavilion were then flung open and the King appeared at the head of a procession consisting of all Anna's pupils and 'a formidable staff of noble dowagers – his sisters, half-sisters and aunts'.

The King shook hands with both Anna and Louis and explained that he was about to confer a distinction on her for her 'courage and conduct at the deathbed of his well-beloved child'. Having instructed her to remain seated (which, as she was sure her dress must be stuck to the chair, she did without demur) Mongkut took the ends of seven threads of cotton, passed them over her head, over the dead child's books and into the hands of his seven eldest sisters. The other ends of each piece of thread he proceeded to wind round Anna's head, much to her embarrassment. 'The whole affair was ridiculous, and I was inclined to feel a little ashamed of the distinction when I reflected on the absurd figure I must have cut with my head in a string like a grocer's parcel.' Louis stared in amazement as the King waved some gold coins in the air, dribbled some water at Anna's feet out of a conch shell and finally placed in her lap a small silk bag containing a title of nobility and the deeds to a tract of land.

> My estate was in the district of Lopburi and I found that to reach it I must perform a tedious journey overland through a wild dense jungle on the back of an elephant. So, with wise munificence, I left it to the people, tigers, elephants, rhinoceroses, wild boars, armadillos and monkeys to enjoy unmolested and untaxed, while I continued to pursue the even tenor of a 'school-marm's' way, unagitated by my honorary title.

★ ★ ★ ★

Readers of Anna's books are struck by two curious omissions. Firstly she makes no mention of acquiring any real friends while she was in Siam. There was no shortage of European or American company in Bangkok had she sought it out; diplomats, missionaries, traders, and very often their families too, yet she admits to being close to none of them. Once again it seems that her uncertain grasp of the social pecking order made it difficult to know just whose company it was appropriate for her to seek. Missionaries and traders, she suspected, should be well below her level, yet diplomats and their families might well spurn her approach. She must have been painfully lonely.

The second curiosity, which can probably be explained by the fact that she was a 'traveller' by necessity and not from choice, was that she seems to have seen very little of Siam during her six years there. The only excursion she mentions making outside Bangkok was when she accompanied Mongkut and some of his children on a river trip, but she reveals neither the destination nor the duration of this jaunt. At some time, though, she does appear to have visited Angkor, or 'Naghkon' Wat – the vast ruined city hidden deep in the jungles of neighbouring Cambodia. Because it had not been 'discovered' by Europeans until 1860, Angkor had not yet achieved the fame that would later lead to its being called the 'Eighth Wonder of the World'. Anna therefore had no inkling of the glories that lay ahead of her as, travelling first by boat and then overland on elephants, she approached the creeper-festooned walls of the ancient city.

> In the heart of this lonely region we found architectural remains of such exceeding grandeur that we were overwhelmed with astonishment and admiration. We marvelled at the work of a race of whose existence the Western nations know nothing, who have no name in history, yet who builded in a style surpassing in boldness of conception, grandeur of proportions and delicacy of design, the best works of the modern world. Stupendous, beautiful, yet slowly crumbling among the wild plantains and the pagan lotuses and lilies, it is more impressive in its loneliness, more elegant and animated in its grace than aught that Greece and Rome have left us, and addresses us with a significance all the sadder and more solemn for the desolation and barbarism which surround it.

Since she neither identifies the 'we' nor gives any date to her visit it is impossible to know for sure, but it seems likely that hers were the first British eyes ever to widen in amazement at the wonders of Angkor. It is one of her most endearing qualities that she was able to admire without reservation the glories of an alien civilisation – many of her contemporaries would merely have dismissed them as the ill-conceived creations of an ignorant and pagan people.

*   *   *   *

The least favourite of Anna's duties were those involved in being the King's secretary. 'His moods were so fickle and unjust, his temper so tyrannical, that it seemed impossible to please him.' Sometimes he would expect her to add eight or nine hours of secretarial work to her daily teaching routine and eventually she rebelled – not by refusing to work, but by asking for an increase in salary. The conditions of her original employment had included the assurance that if she gave satisfaction this would be increased at the end of a year. In fact she had been in Siam for more than three years before she 'ventured to remind the King of his promise'. She obviously picked the wrong moment. Mongkut told her bluntly that not only had she not given satisfaction but that she was difficult and unmanageable.

> You come into my presence every day with some petition, some case of hardship or injustice, and you demand 'your Majesty shall most kindly investigate and cause redress to be made', and I have granted to you because you are important to me for translations and so forth. And now you declare you must have an increase of salary. Must you have everything in this world?

It was in March 1867 that the King and the governess had their most spectacular disagreement; the one that would indirectly lead to Anna's leaving Siam. Mongkut was involved in some particularly delicate negotiations with the French over the question of Cambodia, the strains of which were making him more touchy and irascible than ever. French colonial expansion in South-east Asia had reached alarming proportions with the secession of part of Cochin China (now Vietnam) to the French in 1862 and the subsequent adoption of Cambodia as a French protectorate in 1864. The King of Cambodia had previously paid homage to Siam, and while Mongkut was reluctant to relinquish his influence over his neighbour he was also anxious not to come into open conflict with the French.

It had taken Mongkut and his advisors three years to formulate a satisfactory compromise which he was now ready to present to the French. It stated that he would agree to renounce his own claims to sovereignty over Cambodia if the French would give up their claims to the three Cambodian provinces on the Siamese border. He spent several days concocting and dictating to Anna the terms and conditions under which he was prepared to proceed. In the course of writing out the final draft of Mongkut's letter Anna adjusted the King's wording in several places to make it read more fluently. Although she had frequently found this to be necessary in the past, Mongkut had either not noticed or not minded. So sensitive was this situation, though, and so tightly were his nerves stretched in his anxiety to get it right, that Mongkut not only noticed her alterations but construed them as an attempt to alter his meaning and thereby to influence international affairs. In short he accused Anna of being a spy.

Eventually this row, like all the others, blew over. The new treaty with France was signed by Mongkut's envoys in Paris in July 1867 and once it was out of the way the King forgot all about his suspicions. But by then Anna had had enough. Her health broke down, and for a while she was so ill that the British doctor who attended her thought she might die.

When good Dr Campbell gave me the solemn warning all my trouble seemed to cease, and but for one sharp pang for my children – one in England, the other in Siam – I should have derived pure and perfect pleasure from the prospect of eternal rest, so weary was I of my tumultuous life in the East. Though in the end I regained my strength in a measure, I was no longer able to comply with the pitiless exactions of the king. And so I decided to return to England.

*   *   *   *

It is difficult to assess the extent to which the constant friction between Anna and Mongkut was the result of her masquerade. But that it played some part is beyond doubt. The strain of sustaining her adopted role made her as brittle and touchy as he was, and insecurity made her oversensitive to criticism or opposition; the contradictions in her behaviour disconcerted the King and accentuated his own perverseness. He was very ready to acknowledge her qualities as a teacher and he responded warmly to her appreciation of the art, literature and architecture of his country and to her respect for his religion. But he could never forgive her for her constant interference in his domestic affairs and he could never understand her refusal to accept his absolute authority.

The mixture of respect and exasperation with which he regarded her were evident in his reaction to her announcement that she was leaving Siam. For several weeks, the King refused to speak to her. Yet when it came to the moment of farewell he made her a touching little speech.

Mam, you much beloved by our common people, and all inhabitants of palace and royal children. Every one is in affliction of your departure. It shall be because you must be a good and true lady. I am often angry on you, and lose my temper, though I have large respect for you. But nevertheless you ought to know you are a difficult woman, and more difficult than generality. But you will forget, and come back to my service, for I have more confidence on you every day. Goodbye.

*   *   *   *

Anna never went back to Siam. On her return to England she was reunited with her daughter Avis whom she had not seen for nearly six years. After settling Louis in a boarding school in Ireland, Anna and Avis went to America. Avis married an American and Anna spent the rest of her life there and in Canada.

Her first book, *The English Governess at the Siamese Court*, was published in America in 1870, and the success of this prompted her to write a second, *The Romance of Siamese Harem Life*, in 1873. Both books contain whole chapters of engrossing social, architectural and historical detail, touching personal anecdotes and vivid descriptions of the intimate private world of the royal palace, the veracity of which have never been called into question. Sadly, though, she destroyed her credibility as a historian by embroidering an intrinsically fascinating tale with unnecessary and inaccurate additions. Her reasons for this were purely commercial – now, as before, she was merely trying to earn her living, and generous helpings of skulduggery and scandal have always done wonders for book sales. Fortunately for her peace of mind and for her pocket, the historians did not latch on to her transgressions until many years after her death, and she enjoyed several years as something of a celebrity in American literary circles. Her third and last book, *Life and Travels in India*, was published in 1884 but, perhaps because the Americans were not very interested in India or perhaps because this time she omitted the scandals, it was less well received.

King Mongkut died in 1868, just a year after Anna's departure, and was succeeded by his son Chulalongkorn who would earn himself a reputation for wisdom and tolerance that equalled that of his father. One of his first acts as King would be to abolish the practice of prostration that had so enraged his former governess. Although Anna never went back to Siam, Louis did return there in 1880. After several years as what can only be described as a mercenary soldier in the service of his old playmate Chulalongkorn, he made a fortune in the teak business before retiring to England just before the Great War and dying in the post-war flu epidemic in 1919. Anna herself died in Nova Scotia in 1915.

It is ironic that, although her books were banned in Siam (later Thailand) for many years because the Siamese held her responsible for the slanderous depiction of Mongkut, they are now readily available there, while in Britain they are all out of print and largely forgotten. The western historians who consider that her lapses place her beneath their contempt are obviously less forgiving than their Thai counterparts. One has even gone so far as to accuse her of 'distorting history for three generations'.

But if she was to some extent a fraud, she was also a very remarkable woman. It took real courage for a solitary Englishwoman to live and work in a strange country with only her child for company, and it took real courage (it still does) to stand up to the Supreme King of Siam. Her concern and affection for the people of Siam were genuine and deep; her abhorrence of slavery, her espousal of the cause of the women and children of the royal household, and her refusal to be overawed by those whose authority had never before been challenged prove that she was not afraid to stand up for her own rights and for those of others whom she considered oppressed. Most admirable of all, though, was her complete lack of religious or cultural prejudice, a refreshing contrast indeed to the attitudes that prevailed among her contemporaries – even those of the most impeccable breeding.

CHAPTER · THREE

'MERE MORTALS AND ENGLISHWOMEN'
· *Amelia Edwards* ·

n the evening of 29 November 1873, the door of the great dining
room of Shepheards' Hotel in Cairo opened to admit two late-
comers. The buzz of conversation and the discreet clink of china
were still for a moment as all eyes turned to look at the new arrivals. They
were seen to be two middle-aged Englishwomen, and their appearance –
travel-stained, weary, and by their own admission, considerably sunburnt –
raised not a few eyebrows among the diners. The first of the two ladies (for
ladies they undoubtedly were) was an imposing figure, grey-haired and
ample-bosomed, who seemed not the least embarrassed at being late,
unexpected and unsuitably dressed. Indeed she seemed to gain some
amusement from thus finding herself the focus of so much curiosity. Her
companion was not embarrassed either – but only because she knew that no
one ever paid any attention to a shadow.

Once they had taken their seats at one of the few unoccupied tables the
curious diners resumed their meals and the noise level returned to its
customary hum. Such was the nature of Cairo society that within two days
everything there was to know about these newcomers would be known –
who they were, where they had come from and what they were doing in
Egypt.

Not that it was any secret. Indeed the imposing lady was very ready to
tell the world all about herself: that is if the world did not know already. For
she was none other than The Writer, Miss Amelia Blandford Edwards. She
and her companion had just arrived from Alexandria. They had not dressed
for dinner because their luggage was still on its way from the station, and,
in truth (she was good at the throwaway line), they had drifted to Egypt
quite by accident. Wet weather had pursued them throughout a sketching
tour of Europe and they had taken refuge in Cairo as they might, in other
circumstances, have taken refuge in the Burlington Arcade – to get out of
the rain.

This little tale, and the manner of its telling, contained a wealth of pointers which would enable the listener neatly to categorise Miss Edwards. She had travelled to Egypt on the spur of the moment – therefore she was not one of the carefully organised and already despised Cook's Tourists, but an independent and imaginative traveller wealthy enough to be able to indulge a distinctly expensive whim. A prolonged summer sketching tour of Europe indicated both a lover of culture and a practised wielder of that most ladylike of implements, the drawing pencil. And the casual reference to London's most exclusive shopping arcade hinted at an easy familiarity with the haunts of the social élite. The code was understood by everyone – but not resented even by the less privileged. The social lines were well drawn among the sizeable expatriate community of Egypt, and like was much happier in the company of like.

But if for the sake of convention Amelia Edwards was prepared to confess to a whim, she was not by nature a drifter. At forty-one years of age, she was a lady not only of independent mind and independent means but also of considerable intelligence. Her father, a military man, had fought with Wellington in the Peninsular War and her mother came from a family of respected Irish lawyers. While they had been alive, Amelia had been content to remain at home in London, developing her not inconsiderable talents as a writer and literary journalist. She had published four novels, books on English and French history and a volume of poetry, and was a frequent contributor to some of the most popular English periodicals. Since the death of her parents when she was thirty, however, she had acquired a distinct taste for travel.

Together with her companion – the shadowy figure whom, in over 800 pages of travelogue, Amelia would only ever identify as 'L' – she had toured the capital cities of Europe. She had 'done' Florence and Venice, Heidelberg and Oberammergau, absorbing culture like a sponge and dispensing it in liberal doses to her long-suffering friends on her return. In 1872 the two ladies had spent three months rambling through the *Untrodden Peaks and Unfrequented Valleys* of the Italian Dolomites – a journey which had encouraged Amelia to make the transition from novelist to travel writer.

Egypt, however, was altogether a new experience. Once she had settled on the country as her refuge from the vagaries of the European climate she had immediately resolved to 'do' it as thoroughly as she had 'done' France, Italy, Germany and Switzerland. By way of preparation – for a Writer, and particularly a Travel Writer, must of course always be well-prepared – she had purchased a copy of that incomparable *vade mecum*, Murray's *Handbook to Lower and Upper Egypt*.

Before long it became clear to Amelia that Murray's had nothing but scorn for travellers who 'merely proposed to do the country in the shortest time they could contrive'. Only those who 'intend to do the whole Nile voyage and who can chose their own time' would really benefit from the wealth of information enclosed within its august pages. These elevated mortals were advised to arrive in Egypt in mid-November and remain there till the end of February, going in a *dahabeeyah* as far as the Second Cataract and back. Those who proposed to do the Eastern Tour completely should then leave Egypt at the beginning of March and go by way of Sinai and Petra to Jerusalem. Five or six weeks in Palestine would bring them to Beirut before the end of May.

Amelia's decision was made before she had reached the end of the chapter. There was really no need to consult 'L'. Amelia knew from long experience that her friend would agree to whatever she suggested. But it was already the end of November; if they were to live up to Murray's expectations and complete the Eastern Tour on schedule, there was no time to waste.

*   *   *   *

Scholars, explorers and adventurers had been quick to take advantage of the Napoleonic invasion of Egypt in 1798. Through the first half of the nineteenth century their numbers increased, expeditions up the Nile became larger and more elaborate, and museums in all the capital cities of Europe were soon expanding to accommodate the steady flow of treasures so easily and so arrogantly collected by these mainly amateur archaeologists. With the opening of the Suez Canal in 1869, just four years before Amelia arrived, the country and its wonders had found themselves situated on the main sea route to India. The cities of Alexandria and Cairo had leapt into fashionable prominence, wintering in Egypt became all the rage, the first Cook's Tour up the Nile took place in that same year, and by 1873 the Nile tourist trade was booming.

There is something incongruous in the realisation that, while these tourists were jostling for the best views and being fleeced by quick-witted vendors of more or less genuine souvenirs at one end of the mighty river, explorers were battling through hostile scrub and mountain at the other end, still trying to determine its source. The celebrated meeting between David Livingstone and Henry Morton Stanley had taken place only two years before in 1871. Dr Livingstone had died in the course of his search for that source just six months before Amelia arrived in Egypt in search of fine weather. As she bustled about Cairo making plans for her journey, word of his death had not yet reached the outside world.

*   *   *   *

The first of Amelia's plans involved the hiring of a *dahabeeyah*, the shallow, flat-bottomed river boats adapted for either sailing or rowing, in which they would travel up the Nile. The negotiations gave the ladies their first insight into the colourful world of Egyptian business dealing.

> The miseries of dahabeeyah-hunting are keener by far than the miseries of house-hunting. Dahabeeyahs are given to changing their places, which houses do not do; and one gets into an appalling state of confusion when attempting to weigh the advantages or disadvantages of boats with six cabins and boats with eight, boats provided with canteen and boats without; boats than can pass the cataract and boats that can't; boats that are only twice as dear as they ought to be and boats with that defect six times multiplied.

Realising, perhaps, that she was not blessed with the 'abnormal amount of patience' that Murray's warned would be essential for anyone wishing to organise their own travel arrangements, Amelia promptly hired a *dragoman* (literally 'translator') to take over all negotiations on her behalf and went sight-seeing instead.

Although she herself would have argued hotly to the contrary, Amelia Edwards does not really belong in the front rank of 'Victorian Lady Travellers'. Compared with some of her more intrepid sisters, she was a mere Tourist. Yet she brought to her touring a curiosity and a dedication that lifted her far above the crowds she so despised. When she arrived in Cairo she admitted to having no oriental experience or knowledge whatever; but that was a situation that would not last long.

At the end of ten days she could look with satisfaction at the sixty pages of Murray's Handbook devoted to the Egyptian capital and its immediate environs and know that she and 'L' had seen nearly everything they mentioned. Including, of course, the Pyramids – although by now she had her own ideas about the right and the wrong way to 'do' the sights of Egypt.

> It must be understood that we did not go to *see* the Pyramids. We only went to look at them. The sight-seeing of Egypt demands some little reading and organising if one is to appreciate what one sees. We will come again at our leisure when we have been up the Nile and back and acquired some practical understanding of the arts and architecture of those far-off days.

They arrived back from Giza to be met by the *dragoman*, Talhamy, with the good news that everything was ready. Their difficulties over the selection of the right-sized *dahabeeyah* had been solved by their decision to 'throw in our lot with three other travellers'. It was a brave decision – but Amelia was at pains to explain that their future companions were not just anybody. One of them, Andrew MacCallum, was already known to her. 'The other two, friends of his, are on their way out from Europe and are not expected in

Cairo for another week,' she explained, adding rather nervously, 'We know nothing of them but their names.' Amelia and 'L' were to set out ahead of the others in the *dahabeeyah* while MacCallum waited in Cairo for his friends. When they arrived they would take the train to Rhoda, the ultimate point of the Nile railway about 180 miles south of Cairo, where the whole party would meet up in two weeks' time.

On the morning of 9 December 1873 Amelia and 'L' took possession of the boat that would be their home for the next seven months.

> We are on board, and have shaken hands with the captain and are as busy as bees; for there are cabins to put in order, flowers to arrange, and a hundred little things to be seen to. It is wonderful what a few books and roses, an open piano and a sketch or two will do. In a few minutes the comfortless hired look has vanished and the 'Philae' wears an aspect as cosy and home-like as if she had been occupied for a month.

Although Amelia could, sometimes, laugh at her own snobbery, it was none the less real for that. There was a very definite hierarchy among travellers at this time and, as Amelia herself wrote, 'The people in *dahabeeyahs* despise Cook's tourists; those who are bound for the Second Cataract look down with lofty compassion on those whose ambition extends only to the First; and travellers who engage their boat by the month hold their heads a trifle higher than those who contract for the trip.' The right connections and acquaintances were very important to Amelia; she was as proud of belonging to the social and intellectual élite as she was of being British, and she would never have dreamed of subjecting herself to the uncomfortable bustle of a Cook's Tour. The luxury of a private *dahabeeyah* was far more her style. And the *Philae* was certainly luxurious. The lower deck comprised a cabin for each of the passengers and a separate cabin at the stern for storing the gentlemen's guns, the ladies' parasols, and the contents of the party's wine cellar. The main room, situated in the centre of the boat, was a spacious saloon with panelled walls and ceiling painted in white picked out with gold, furnished with bookcases, writing tables, drinks cabinets and divans as well as the dining table and the piano. Brightly coloured carpets covered the floors, scarlet and orange curtains matched the chair covers and vases of fresh flowers were placed on each table every day. The upper deck formed an *al fresco* drawing room, open to the air on all sides but fully shaded by an awning during the day. It was furnished with lounge-chairs, tables and oriental rugs and was ideally situated to give the passengers the best possible view of the passing scenery in the greatest possible comfort.

Because the *Philae* was a sailing vessel when the wind blew and a rowing boat when it did not, it required a sizeable crew. Amelia described the twelve sailors in some amazement as being 'of all shades from yellowish bronze to a hue not far removed from black; and though at the first mention of it nothing more incongruous can well be imagined than a sailor in petticoats and turban, yet these men in their loose blue gowns, bare feet and white muslin turbans looked not only picturesque, but dressed exactly as they should be.' 'Our equipment', as Amelia chose to put it, 'was completed by the *Reis* or captain, the steersman, the *dragoman*, head cook, assistant cook, two waiters and the boy who cooked for the crew.' The two ladies therefore made their stately way to Rhoda with an entourage of twenty souls.

Murray's *Handbook* was far from being Amelia's only reading matter. The *Philae*'s bookshelves were groaning under the weight of volumes on Egyptian history, ancient monuments and hieroglyphics. As they drifted slowly southwards she studied Herodotus and Vivant Denon, Champollion, Mariette and Bunsen. ('L', if Amelia is to be believed, spent most of her time knitting.) By the time they stepped ashore at Beni Suef, seven days after leaving Cairo, she was confident enough of her subject to have laid down a plan for the entire journey.

The general rule of Nile travellers was to hurry up the river as fast as possible, leaving the ruins to be seen on the way back. But Miss Edwards knew that was wrong. 'The land of Egypt is a Great Book,' she solemnly lectured the bemused captain, 'not very easy reading under any circumstances, but quite difficult enough already without the added puzzlement of being read backwards.' For this reason, she added, she intended to visit some of the oldest sites on the way south.

What Amelia did not understand, and all her learned books forgot to tell her, was that it was not by accident that most travellers did their sightseeing on the way back. The prevailing wind during the early months of winter blew from the north. It was wise to take advantage of this wind while travelling south to make as much progress under sail as possible. Every windy day wasted at a mooring meant, in all probability, a calm day ahead when the sail would be useless. On the return journey the wind would be irrelevant since they would be travelling with the current. They could therefore afford to stop for as long as they liked wherever they liked, secure in the knowledge that the current would still be flowing in the same direction the following day and every day thereafter. The captain, however, knew his place too well to presume to argue with her. When she insisted on spending a second day at Beni Suef he just shrugged his shoulders, lay down in the shade and went to sleep.

Inevitably the wind, which had been blowing strongly for three days, fell at precisely the moment Amelia decided she was ready to leave Beni Suef.

The alternative source of power therefore had to be brought into action.

> Coming on deck we found nine of our poor fellows harnessed to a rope like barge-horses, towing the huge boat against the current. This sight jarred somehow with the placid beauty of the scenery. We got used to it, as one gets used to everything, in time; but it looked like slave's work and shocked our English notions disagreeably.

It never occurred to her that she might in any way be responsible for their added burden.

She was to find that her English notions were disagreeably shocked on several occasions as they made their way south. The antiquities were quite wonderful. She was entirely happy to spend days poking about in ruins, picking up shards or sketching in the shade of her white parasol. But present-day Egypt was harder to take. There had been nothing in the slums of Europe's capitals or the peasant villages of the Dolomites to prepare her for the poverty and wretchedness of the rural towns along the Nile.

By chance they reached the town of Minieh on market day, and what had started out as a pleasant little stroll through the streets became a procession of horror. The houses which she had fondly imagined would be picturesque or quaint turned out to be little more than windowless mud prisons in trodden lanes of dust. When they reached the central square they found it thronged with 'ten or twelve thousand natives of all ages whose faces were sullen, ignorant and unfriendly'. In mounting horror Amelia noticed that roughly one person in twelve seemed to be 'blind of an eye' (she was not yet familiar with the effects of that scourge of the Nile, ophthalmia); that even the 'better classes' were shabbily dressed, and that the poorest of all were 'simply encrusted with dirt and sores and swarming with vermin'. She turned and fled back to the *Philae*, her handkerchief pressed to her nose. 'It was so distressing', she wrote, 'that one would willingly go miles out of the way rather than witness such suffering without the power of alleviating it.'

It was a clear case of what the eye does not see, the heart does not grieve over. Poverty and squalor might touch her heart but they also turned her stomach. Far better to keep them at a distance from where they had a certain colourful charm. For the rest of the journey Amelia would do just that. She made no attempt to get to know the people of Egypt. She did not taste their food or learn their language, and despite Murray's assurances that she would be quite safe, from that moment on she never left the boat without at least two members of the crew as bodyguards 'to make sure the people are kept at a pleasant distance'.

★   ★   ★   ★

'It is Christmas Day,' she wrote a few days later. 'The cooks are up to their eyes in plum pudding, the crew are being treated to a sheep in honour of the occasion, and the new-comers have arrived.' But Amelia was not filled with the spirit of the season. She and 'L' had been extremely comfortable for the past fortnight; they had had the boat and the running of it to themselves and had organised their lives very nicely, thank you. From now on they would have to share not only the accommodation but the decisions with 'four persons' whose likes and dislikes might be very different from their own.

She could not even welcome Andrew MacCallum, a painter of some repute, without the barbed comment that 'he has brought enough frames, canvasses, drawing paper and easels to start a provincial school of art.' His two friends, of whom she was extremely suspicious, turned out to be on their honeymoon. Amelia instantly, and rather sourly, named them the 'Happy Couple'. 'The bridegroom is what the world calls an Idle Man; that is to say he has scholarship, delicate health and leisure. The bride, for convenience, shall be called the Little Lady.' The fourth person, whom one suspects Amelia only mentioned in order to stress the magnitude of the invasion, was the Little Lady's maid. Amelia did not mention her again.

Her penchant for the graphic nickname was such that the unfortunate honeymooners would remain collectively the 'Happy Couple' and individually the 'Idle Man' and the 'Little Lady' for the duration of their Nile voyage. Even MacCallum became, and remained, 'The Painter', while from that moment on she never referred to herself as anything other than 'The Writer'. Poor 'L' never even graduated to 'The Knitter'; she remained simply 'L'.

Sometimes sailing, sometimes tracking, sometimes punting, the *Philae* and its mutually wary passengers progressed slowly southwards. The skies were cloudless, the days warm and the evenings exquisite. When there was no wind, the more energetic among them went ashore and walked on ahead of the straining trackers. When on board The Painter painted, The Writer wrote and read copiously and the Idle Man, who had high hopes of bagging an impressive trophy, kept a keen look out for crocodiles. 'L' and the Little Lady spent a lot of time feeding the unfortunate rabbits and flocks of assorted poultry cooped up on the after-deck waiting for their turn in the pot, much to the amusement of the steersman who, unable to conceive of any other motive, imagined they were fattening them for the table.

As the season advanced the captain enlisted the help of the *dragoman* in trying to rid Amelia of her contrary notions. But although the *dragoman* was braver than the captain, he was no more successful. Amelia's mind was made up.

No *dragoman* could ever be made to understand the importance of historical sequence in a matter of this kind. To him Khufu, Rameses and the Ptolemies are one. As for the monuments, they are all ancient Egyptian and one is just as odd and unintelligible as another. We cannot all be profoundly learned, but we can at least do our best to understand what we see. Some places must be seen on the way up, no matter at what trifling cost of present delay and despite any amount of ignorant opposition.

Fortunately neither The Painter nor the Happy Couple seemed at this stage to resent Amelia's busy management of their schedule, and 'L' had long been written off by her ungrateful friend as being 'culpably indifferent to glory'. So Amelia got her way. And it has to be said that she made the most of it. Although her understanding of modern Egypt was still, and would remain, severely limited, she was developing a veritable passion for its past. 'Many travellers visit the temples merely as a duty', she wrote, 'but I could breakfast, dine and sup on Temples. My appetite is insatiable.' At Denderah she lingered so long over the sculptures that darkness fell and a search party had to be sent out to find her. The Great Temple at Karnak achieved the greatest coup by rendering her speechless.

To describe it is impossible. The scale is too vast, the effect too tremendous, the sense of one's own dumbness and littleness and incapacity too complete and crushing. It empties you not only of words, but of ideas. Others might measure and plan and climb – but I could only look, and be silent.

As far as Aswan Amelia's journey differed very little from the same journey as it is made today. Such differences as there were were of degree rather than fundamental substance. Her boat was a sailing vessel where today's tourists travel in motor launches. Many of the now famous treasures – the Great Ship of Cheops at Giza, the tomb of Tutankhamun at Thebes – still lay undiscovered under millions of tons of sand. But the great sites were there to be explored.

The traveller who reached Aswan in 1874, however, was faced with a substantial obstacle that, within thirty years, would no longer exist – an obstacle that, as far as Amelia was concerned, gave the upper stretches of the Nile an added charm by placing them out of reach of the common tourist. No Cook's steamer and only the cream of Nile *dahabeeyahs* could pass beyond the notorious Aswan Cataract. Amelia was not convinced the *Philae* would make it either – particularly after reading what Murray's *Handbook* had to say on the subject:

The cataract that obstructs the course of the Nile is a succession of rapids, whirlpools and eddies; the ascent and descent of which are incidents in the Nile voyage more exciting than pleasant. Perhaps the best commentary on it is that no one who has gone through it once would willingly do so again, though he might find amusement in watching the process from a nearby rock. For ladies this is decidedly the most agreeable way.

Construction of the first Aswan Dam would start in 1898 and by 1904 travellers would pass the site of the dreaded First Cataract through the tranquil locks of a canal. In 1874, however, the fate of *dahabeeyah* passengers lay in the hands of a gentleman called the Sheikh of the Cataract. Only he had the expertise, the men and the equipment to get them through.

Murray's warned that negotiations with the Sheikh sometimes involved delays of several days. But MacCallum, who had passed this way before, decided that matters could be expedited by a visit to the Governor of Aswan. For once Amelia was willing to relinquish command of the negotiations, and The Painter, 'arrayed in a gorgeous *keffiyeh* [an Arab head-shawl], and armed with the indispensable visiting cane', sprang ashore to call upon the Governor. A couple of hours later the Governor returned the visit, bringing with him the Chief Magistrate and the Judge of Aswan, each attended by his pipe-bearer.

> The guests were received with due ceremony in the saloon. The great men placed themselves on one of the side-divans and The Painter opened the conversation by offering them champagne, claret, port, sherry, curaçao, brandy, whisky and Angostura bitters.

This *faux pas* nearly brought the whole Nile journey to a premature halt. Although the Governor was worldly enough to be amused, both the Magistrate and the Judge were profoundly shocked at the mere mention of these unholy liquors. The situation was saved by the appearance of a waiter with bottles of fizzy lemonade, upon which all three gentlemen fell with undisguised appreciation.

Having seen how the efforts of the others had so nearly ended in disaster, Amelia decided it was time she resumed control of negotiations. But her own attempts were nearly as catastrophic, for her next move was to ask the guests whether it would be possible to visit the slave market in Aswan. The smile vanished from the Governor's face. The Magistrate set down a glass of fizzing lemonade untasted and the Judge dropped his pipe. 'If a shell had burst in the saloon their consternation could hardly have been greater,' Amelia commented in dismay.

Speaking through the interpreter, the Governor assured her that there was no slavery anywhere in Egypt and that there was certainly not a slave market in Aswan. Amelia hastened to explain that they had been told in Cairo on excellent authority that slaves were still bought and sold in Aswan, and that their object was not to satisfy their own idle curiosity but merely to do some sketching. The three visitors shook their heads and continued to look very grave. The awkward silence that followed showed Amelia that she, too, had committed an enormous blunder and she had the grace to admit to being very embarrassed. She also, for once, had cause to be extremely grateful to the Little Lady who rather incongruously sat herself at the piano and played the liveliest thing she could remember, which happened to be a Verdi waltz.

For some reason Verdi did the trick. Or maybe it was the third bottle of lemonade. Governor, Magistrate and Judge departed half an hour later promising to use their influence with the Sheikh of the Cataract to speed things along. The party then dispersed to entertain themselves till the moment for the ascent arrived.

The Painter, set on a little solitude, disappeared with his easel, while 'L' and the Little Lady announced they would devote their time to letter writing. That left The Writer with a difficult choice. She had firmly bracketed herself with the two gentlemen as the only active participants in the journey. To remain on the boat would be to lay herself open to the charges of passivity she regularly but ever so gently levelled at the other ladies. The alternative, however, was to accompany the Idle Man on an expedition that she knew would play havoc with her dignity. The decision made, she hid her apprehension under a cloak of disdain.

> The Writer and the Idle Man boldly mounted camels and rode out into the desert. This outing figures as the crowning achievement of every Cook's tourist. Arabs themselves take good care never to ride on a camel if they can help it, performing their journeys much more expeditiously and pleasantly on donkeys. But for the impressionable traveller, a ride on an Assuan camel is de rigueur. It is a most unpleasant experience. You know that the animal hates you from the moment you first walk round him wondering where and how to begin the ascent of his hump. He swears freely at you while you are taking your seat, snarls if you but move in the saddle, and stares angrily if you try to make him move. Should you persevere he tries to bite your feet. If you succeed in taking your seat atop this execrable hunchback you discover that his gait is as abominable as his temper. He has four paces; a short walk like the rolling of a small boat in a choppy sea; a long walk which dislocates every bone in your body; a trot which reduces you to imbecility; and a gallop that is sudden death.

The day after this uncomfortable expedition, the Sheikh of the Cataract made his appearance with a team of labourers. In preparation for the ascent the windows of the *Philae* were shuttered, doors closed and breakables moved to a place of safety just as if she were being prepared for a storm at sea. Given favourable conditions and a measure of good luck the ascent might be made in twelve hours. Conversely, any one of a million little misfortunes could extend this to as much as four days.

Scorning Murray's advice that ladies would be happier to watch from the bank, Amelia took up a position in the prow of the boat to be sure of an uninterrupted view of the proceedings. Her first sight of the rapids that marked the beginning of the cataract convinced her that she would be happier watching from the saloon; 'a chain of small islets barred the way, while the current, divided into three or four headlong torrents between them came rushing down the slope and reunited at the bottom in one tumultuous race.'

As they approached 'this hill of moving water', the Sheikh, 'a flat-faced, fishy-eyed old Nubian' continued to smoke imperturbably. At the last moment, and without removing his pipe from his mouth, he delivered the one word 'Forward'. Instantly the rocks on all sides swarmed with men; ropes were thrown from the rocks to the boat, other ropes were thrown from the deck to the shore, and soon upwards of a hundred men were ranged along them. The Sheikh gave a signal and, 'to a wild chanting accompaniment and a movement like a barbaric Sir Roger de Coverley dance', the men began to pull. Considering the volume of water flowing against them and the size of the boat (over a hundred feet long and nearly thirty feet wide) their task seemed an impossible one. But almost imperceptibly the *Philae* started to move. For two hours the men chanted and pulled; white water crashed against the bows, the anxious passengers in the saloon lurched and jolted, the ropes strained – and finally the boat swung with a rush over the top of the rapid and into a pool of comparatively smooth water.

This performance would have to be repeated six times before they reached the top of the Cataract. On the second rapid one of the tow ropes broke – the twenty men along it toppled over like dominoes on the rocks and the *Philae* swung round broadside to the current. Mercifully the other ropes held, but the incident proved too much for the pullers. They put down their ropes and went home. The Sheikh, not the least embarrassed by this, promised that they would return in the morning, and Amelia and her companions, slightly bewildered, were left moored midway between two rapids.

By noon the following day not a single man had reappeared. Amelia protested. The Sheikh just smoked and shook his head; 'in the Cataract as elsewhere, there were lucky and unlucky days, days when men felt inclined to work and days when they felt disinclined. Today, as it happened, they felt disinclined.'

Once again The Painter stepped in. Being a practical man, he had compiled a little vocabulary of choice Arab maledictions which he carried in his note-book for reference when needed. The rest of the party had laughed at this much as they laughed at his pocket revolver which was never loaded or his brand new fowling piece which he was never known to fire. But the Sheikh of the Cataract had gone too far. 'The fatuity of his smile would have exasperated the meekest of men; and our Painter was not the meekest of men,' Amelia explained. So MacCallum whipped out his book, selected an appropriate quotation and delivered it to the Sheikh.

> The Sheikh sprang to his feet as if he had been shot – vowed the Philae might stay where she was until doomsday for all he cared – bounded into his own rickety little boat and rowed away, leaving us to our fate. We stood aghast. It was all over with us – we should never see Abou [Abu] Simbel now. What was to be done? Must the Sheikh be defied, or propitiated? Should we appeal to the Governor? Or should we immolate The Painter? The majority were for immolating The Painter.

Their second night moored in the Cataract was even less comfortable than the first. The rushing tumult of the river through the nearby rapids made sleep hard to find and the atmosphere among the passengers was hardly more soothing. The Writer was loudly reproachful, The Painter defiant and the Happy Couple acutely embarrassed. 'L' tiptoed about trying to keep out of the way.

> To everyone's surprise, and immense relief, the Sheikh reappeared at sunrise the following morning, wreathed in smiles and accompanied by twice as many men as before. Declaring that The Painter was his brother, that we were all his dearest friends and that there was nothing he would not do for us, he ordered his men to the ropes. From dawn till dusk they heaved and sweated until, as the sun set and the afterglow faded from the sky, the Philae rounded the last bend, negotiated the last rapid and slipped into level water. Neither I nor anyone else ever again made light of The Painter's repertory of abuse.

The top of the First Cataract marked the spot where, a century later, the Aswan High Dam would be built to regulate the sometimes disastrous seasonal fluctuations of the river. Since the 1960s the remaining three hundred miles of Amelia's southward journey have been submerged in the waters of Lake Nasser. The first archaeological site that Amelia and her party visited above the cataract was the little island of Philae, from which their *dahabeeyah* took its name. And it was here, among the exquisite statues, colonnades and courtyards of the temples dedicated to Isis, that Amelia's attitude to the antiquities of Egypt underwent a fundamental change.

At Giza and Luxor, Karnak and Denderah, and at every other site below the First Cataract, vendors of souvenirs had seemed as much part of the scene as the antiquities themselves. Although she had prided herself on being less gullible than most as to the authenticity of the statues and artefacts on offer, Amelia had haggled for 'genuine antikas' with a clear conscience. At Sakkarah she admitted to having 'learned to rummage among dusty sepulchres with no more compunction than would have befitted a professional body-snatcher'. At Memphis she had cheerfully gathered 'many curious fragments of glass and pottery, and part of an engraved bronze Apis', while at Elephantine near Aswan she had collected several pieces of inscribed terracotta from what looked like an ancient rubbish heap.

Philae was different. The fact that it was above rather than below the First Cataract had protected it from all but the most determined Nile travellers. The site had indeed been pillaged; pavements had been torn up by ancient treasure-seekers, a complete obelisk had been removed and transported to Cairo and thence to England by Giovanni Belzoni in 1818, and stones from the temple walls had been removed and used as building materials by local villagers. But instead of an air of exhausted dereliction, the temples of Philae had 'a freshness and a fairness that makes us believe that the work is not marred but arrested'. It was as if the masons and sculptors had just laid down their tools for a moment and would be back directly to carry on their work. Here there were no crowds of 'antika' sellers clamouring for her custom, no pedlars of papyri, no beggars of 'baksheesh'. 'The Holy Island of Philae', wrote Amelia, 'beautiful, lifeless, a thing of the far past, with all its wealth of sculpture, painting, history, poetry, tradition' seemed to sleep, as yet undisturbed.

The contrast opened Amelia's eyes to the devastating effects not just of tourism but also of scholarship. It seemed to be the fate of every monument, great or small, to have the tourist carve it all over with names and dates; to have the student of Egyptology sponging away all trace of original colour by taking 'wet paper squeezes', and to have the 'collector' buy and carry off everything of value that he could lay his hands on. 'The work of destruction goes on apace,' she mourned. And it was not just foreigners who were to blame. The archaeological wonders of the Nile had no official protection – indeed the government seemed to think that chunks of Egypt's heritage were fair exchange for international interest and investment. On an individual level, too, for every British, Italian, French or American visitor keen to acquire a piece of Egypt's history for his museum or for his drawing room there was an Arab ready, for a price, to show him where to find it.

The temples of Abu Simbel, Amelia's ultimate goal, were under threat of a different kind. A hundred and eighty miles south of Philae, their existence had first been brought to the notice of European archaeology by the Swiss explorer Johann Burckhardt in 1812. The two temples had been hewn out of the rock faces of adjacent hillsides divided by a deep cleft. Over the centuries a great cataract of sand, narrow at the top and opening out like a fan at the bottom, had poured through this cleft, slanting down across the façades of the temples on either side. When Burckhardt arrived, the great drift had covered the main doorway of the Great Temple, itself over twenty feet high, to a depth of more than thirty feet. The drift had been partially cleared by Belzoni in 1817, by Lepsius in 1844 and again by Mariette in 1869. But each time the sands had crept inexorably back. Abu Simbel became known as the 'elusive wonder' of the Nile.

As Amelia and her party approached the site in 1874 they had no way of knowing how far the sand would have encroached in the five years since it had last been cleared. But the uncertainty added spice to her anticipation. Although the efforts of a 'mere mortal and Englishwoman' could not hope to turn back the tide, at least she could record and sketch whatever was left uncovered before the 'elusive wonders' once again disappeared.

From Philae southwards the climate had become noticeably warmer and more sultry. It was now too hot to sit on the upper deck during the day, even with the awning in place, and the energetic Miss Edwards was forced to admit that 'to take a walk on the shore became a duty rather than a pleasure.' The surrounding desert, never more than half a mile away from the river on either side and sometimes as close as six yards, was an oppressive presence; it deprived The Painter of material for his pictures and made 'L' and the Little Lady sigh for the lusher banks of the Lower Nile. The Idle Man was having trouble hiding his disappointment at the complete absence of crocodiles – and his frustration was intensified by the sight of a homeward-bound *dahabeeyah* drifting northwards 'garlanded with crocodiles from stem to stern'. But Amelia seemed oblivious to the subdued atmosphere among her companions. As they rounded the last bend in the river before Abu Simbel, just before midnight on 31 January, she could hardly contain her excitement.

'Finally the corner was rounded and the Great Temple stood straight before us. Though it was night the façade, sunk in the mountainside like a huge picture in a mighty frame, was now quite plain to see.' After this first glimpse of the wonders of Abu Simbel, 'L' and the Happy Couple went straight to bed, much to Amelia's disgust.

But The Painter and The Writer had no patience to wait till morning. Almost before the mooring rope could be made fast they had jumped ashore and begun climbing the bank. They went and stood at the feet of the colossi; and on the threshold of that vast portal. The great statues towered above their heads. The river glittered like steel in the far distance. There was a keen silence in the air;

and towards the east the Southern Cross was rising. The time, the place, even the sound of their own voices, seemed unreal. They felt as if the whole scene must fade with the moonlight, and vanish before morning.

If the scene was less ethereal in the sunlight of the following morning, it was even more impressive. Awed by the immensity of the statues, the beauty and complexity of the wall-sculptures and the painted rock chambers, the party wandered round the temples of Abu Simbel 'lost in wonder, like rustics at a fair'. It was immediately obvious that the shifting sands were indeed on the move again; two of the seventy-foot high statues were already buried to the waist and the floor of the Great Temple was covered to a depth of two feet. Its relentless advance gave an added impetus both to The Writer's pen and The Painter's brush. Oblivious to the blistering heat, heedless of the clouds of flies that drowned in their watercolours and the sand that filled their hair, their eyes and their food, they pitched their little sketching tents and started to record the wonders of Abu Simbel for posterity.

According to Murray's *Handbook* it was customary for *dahabeeyah* passengers to set aside one, or at the most two, days for the exploration of the temples of Abu Simbel. When neither The Writer nor The Painter showed any signs of being ready to move after a week, rumblings of discontent were heard to emanate from the crew quarters of the *Philae*. The men had nothing to do, explained the *dragoman*. The Painter had the answer. The face of the northernmost statue of Rameses was still disfigured by the plaster left on it when a cast had been taken for the British Museum by Mr Hay fifty years ago: the crew of the *Philae* would restore it. Under Amelia's watchful eye the bemused sailors found themselves scraping off lumps of plaster and disguising the blotches by dabbing them with bits of sponge soaked in black coffee.

No sooner had occupation been found for the crew, however, than Amelia's hitherto docile companions rebelled. The Happy Couple announced they wanted to continue south to the Second Cataract in search of a change of scene and maybe, finally, some crocodiles. Since the *dahabeeyah* was their only accommodation, the group could not split up. Reluctantly Amelia agreed to go on to Wadi Halfeh on condition they spend at least as long again at Abu Simbel on the way back. But as far as she was concerned it was a waste of time. 'If a traveller pressed for time asked me whether he should continue to the Second Cataract I should recommend him to turn back at Abou Simbel,' she wrote crossly. 'The trip takes between four and seven days; the forty miles of river that have to be twice traversed are the dullest on the Nile; the Second Cataract is but a barren edition of the first and the view has none of the beauty.'

She did admit, however, that this last navigable stretch of the river had an interest 'beyond and apart from that of beauty'. To reach this point they had travelled nearly 1000 miles against the stream, but as yet no one knew for sure how many more thousands of miles of the mighty river lay between the Second Cataract at Wadi Halfeh and the Great Lakes of Victoria and Tanganyika discovered by Speke and Burton. Nor indeed how far again beyond the lakes might prove to be the still undiscovered source. Even to reach Khartoum, 700 miles south of Wadi Halfeh, involved a 'short cut' away from the rapid-strewn river and across what Murray's described as flat and uninteresting country – a gruelling camel-trek that would take upwards of six weeks. Amelia was not tempted, as other more adventurous souls might have been, to step into the unknown. Once she had paid her respects to the unmapped void she was impatient to get back to Abu Simbel.

*   *   *   *

When they regained their old mooring Amelia was more than a little put out to find a fleet of no less than five *dahabeeyahs* rocking gently by the bank, and several new sketching tents in occupation of 'their' ground. For three days she had to put up with 'arrivals and departures, exchanges of visits, exhibitions of sketches and sociabilities of various kinds', into all of which the Happy Couple and The Painter entered with great gusto. The other travellers, however, seemed to agree with Murray's that a day or two at Abu Simbel was sufficient, and by the end of three days the *Philae* and her passengers once more had the place entirely to themselves.

By now it was mid-February and the Nile tourist season was well advanced. If the Idle Man had not chanced to catch sight of his first crocodile just as the last of the other *dahabeeyahs* was gliding out of sight, it seems probable that Amelia would have been deprived of her moment of glory. The poor fellow had almost ceased to believe that there were any crocodiles in Egypt at all and, prompted by the Little Lady, had been on the point of suggesting that the *Philae* should follow the other *dahabeeyahs* northwards. A thrashing of water on the far side of the river, a dash across in the little rowing boat, and the sight of fresh footprints in the sand were enough to rekindle all his enthusiasm. 'He flew at once to arms,' wrote Amelia. 'He caused a shallow grave to be dug for himself a few yards from the spot, then went and lay in it for hours together, morning after morning under the full blaze of the sun – flat, patient, alert, with his gun ready cocked,' and for some unexplained reason, with a copy of a London magazine, the *Pall Mall Budget*, stuffed up the back of his jacket.

It was all most satisfactory. The Painter was in the middle of a master-piece and determined to finish it before leaving, 'L' and the Little Lady were far too timid to make any suggestions at all, let alone unpopular ones, and now the only person who might have tried to make her move on was fully and happily occupied. The Writer was therefore free to write, sketch or merely wander around the temples at will. 'Abou Simbel is a wonderful place to be alone in,' she wrote, 'a place in which the very darkness and silence are old, and in which Time himself seems to have fallen asleep.'

It was on the fifth day after their return from Wadi Halfeh that 'an event occurred that roused us to an unwonted pitch of excitement and kept us at high pressure through the rest of our time'. The *dragoman* rang the bell on the *Philae* to announce that luncheon was served. The Idle Man, who was still waiting for his crocodile to reappear, dug himself out of his grave and made his way back across the river, The Writer put away her pencil, shook the sand off her skirt and walked down to the boat where 'L' and the Little Lady were already at table. There was no sign of The Painter. Talhamy rang the luncheon bell a second time and when he still did not reappear the meal was started without him. They had almost finished eating when one of the crew appeared with a pencilled note. 'Pray come immediately,' it read. 'I have found the entrance to a tomb. Please send some sandwiches.'

With a turn of speed quite startling in one usually so dignified, Amelia leapt ashore and bounded up the hill to The Painter's side. His attention had been caught by a long crack running down the face of the rock at the top of a mound of sand not far from the Great Temple. By the time Amelia arrived he had cleared away some of the sand with his hands and uncovered a hole about six inches square through which it was just possible to catch a glimpse of painted walls.

Careful perusal of Murray's *Handbook* intensified their excitement for it made no mention of a temple, tomb or any other structure at this spot. Whatever it was that MacCallum had discovered, it was not something that had recently been reclaimed by the shifting sands. It was a structure, unknown to modern man, that had been buried by the great fan-shaped drift, possibly for as long as 3000 years.

The Idle Man forgot all about crocodiles, 'L' and the Little Lady about their knitting. The entire crew was summoned to the spot, and they began to dig.

All that afternoon, heedless of possible sunstroke, unconscious of fatigue, we toiled on our hands and knees. With a spade or two or a wheelbarrow we could have done wonders, but we had only one small fire-shovel, a birch broom, a couple of charcoal baskets and about twenty pairs of hands. What was wanted in means, however, was made up in method. Some scraped away the sand, some gathered it into baskets, some carried the baskets to the edge of the cliff and emptied them into the river. The Idle Man distinguished himself by scooping out a channel where the slope was steepest which greatly facilitated the work. Emptied down this shoot and kept continually going, the sand poured off in a steady stream like water.

The opening grew rapidly larger. By sunset the top of a doorway was laid bare, and a large enough space had been cleared below for a member of the crew to be sent in with a candle to check the freshness of the air inside. He emerged to confirm this and Amelia was next to take a look. Having with some difficulty wriggled through the gap she found herself looking down into a small square chamber, measuring about fourteen by twenty feet and still more than half filled by a great slope of sand. There was light enough to see every detail distinctly; the painted frieze running round just under the ceiling and the bas-relief sculptures on the walls 'gorgeous with unfaded colour'.

The following morning the captain of the *Philae* was despatched to the nearest village with orders to bring back fifty able-bodied natives. With their assistance it took only two days to clear the remaining sand from the chamber. The villagers were paid off and the triumphant archaeologists were left in peace to evaluate their discovery. But the excitement was not yet over.

While The Writer busied herself copying the paintings and inscriptions and The Painter measured and surveyed the chamber, the Idle Man set to work probing a hollow space in the centre of one of the outer walls. His fingers suddenly met a solid object buried in the sand. Carefully withdrawing his hand he found to his amazement that he was holding a human skull. For the moment he said nothing, but continued to feel around in the sand; his exclamation of surprise when he next withdrew a small clay bowl brought us running to his side. By the end of the afternoon we had uncovered another bowl, a second, smaller skull and the bones of two complete skeletons all in perfect condition. The teeth were sound, the bones wonderfully delicate and brittle, and the smaller skull was as pure and fragile in texture as the cup of a water-lily.

Their imaginations ran riot. Although the skeletons and the bowls were almost certainly modern, there was no knowing what might lie buried beneath them.

We were convinced that what we had found was a mortuary chapel, that the hollow in the wall would lead to a sepulchral chamber, and that at the bottom of it we should find – who could tell what? Mummies perhaps, and sarcophagi and funerary statuettes and jewels and papyri and wonders without end. If modern Nubians at the top, why not ancient Egyptians at the bottom?

Another week of careful excavation dashed all their great hopes. The hollow in the wall did indeed lead downwards, but only to an empty basement.

The elaborately decorated chamber, which later experts would decide had once been a library, was all that was left of a monumental gateway tower which had been destroyed, probably by an earthquake, during the reign of Rameses II.

> Our mummies melted into thin air and we were left with no excuse to carry on the excavations. In vain we told ourselves that the discovery of the remains of a large tower was of far greater importance than the finding of a tomb. We had set our hearts on the tomb, and I am afraid we cared less than we ought for the tower.

Amelia's disappointment was short-lived. Although there had been no mummies and no treasure, she had contributed her mite to the exploration of Egypt's antiquities. She – oh, and The Painter too of course – had discovered a perfectly preserved and wonderfully decorated chamber that had been missed by some of the century's greatest archaeologists. Belzoni, Champollion and Lepsius had searched; Amelia Edwards and Andrew MacCallum had found.

But her pride was mixed with sadness. For the discovery made her feel in some way responsible for the fate of all Egypt's antiquities. When The Painter announced that he had written the names of the party and the date of their discovery over the inside of the doorway of their chamber, she knew it would be churlish to protest. But she knew too that this act marked the beginning of the end of the purity they had been so privileged to see. Already the brilliance and freshness of the paintings had been marred by their excavations and the colours blurred where the labourers had leaned their perspiring backs against the walls. Like the naturalist who discovers a rare plant and announces it to the world, knowing that its future will immediately be threatened by the trampling feet of eager followers in his footsteps, Amelia could hear the warning bells ring for her chamber.

> Every day more inscriptions are mutilated, more tombs are rifled, more paintings and sculptures are defaced. The Louvre contains a full-length portrait of Seti I, cut out bodily from the walls of his sepulchre in the Valley of the Tombs of the Kings. The Museums of Berlin, of Turin, of Florence, are rich in spoils which tell their own lamentable tale. When science leads the way, is it wonderful that ignorance should follow?

They left Abu Simbel on 18 February. From now on they would be travelling into the wind so the masts and sails of the *dahabeeyah* were stowed away. The return journey would be accomplished by the strength of their oarsmen and the pull of the current. For a while the party had been united by the excitement of their discoveries at Abu Simbel, but once they had left the scene of their mutual triumph it was not long before their differences resurfaced. The Painter had achieved his masterpiece and was ready to return to Cairo. The Happy Couple plucked up the courage, at last, to admit openly that they were longing to get back to modern civilisation. But Amelia would have none of it. She had laid out her itinerary and she was going to stick to it. And as ever she had her way. 'There are fourteen temples between Abou Simbel and Assuan and we still had many to explore below the cataract. Though they had been twice as many I should not have wished them fewer; I went over them all, took notes of them all and sketched them every one.'

The descent of the Aswan Cataract was far more alarming than the ascent had been, but at least it took only 'one short, sensational half-hour' instead of four struggling days. When the *Philae* emerged from the hair-raising shoot intact except for one broken oar, Amelia could hardly restrain a gleeful chuckle at the sight of a Cook's steamer which had been doing nothing more ambitious than turning round when it had struck a rock and foundered.

In the mêlée that surrounded the wrecked steamer, The Painter suddenly saw his chance. Amongst those offering succour to the stranded Cook's tourists was what Amelia described as 'a noble Duke honeymooning in a steam-tug' – which aristocrat just happened to be an old friend of Mac-Callum's. Within a matter of minutes The Painter had transported his masterpiece, his luggage and all the paraphernalia of his studio from the *Philae* to the ducal launch, and was last seen waving farewell to his erstwhile travelling companions from the stern as the steam-tug 'disappeared gaily in the distance at the rate of twenty miles an hour'.

The Happy Couple were anything but happy to see him go. Tired of temples, tired of drifting slowly down-river with the current but against a determined headwind, and most of all tired of Amelia, there was nothing they would have liked better than to escape with him on his speedy new vessel. As it was, they could anticipate an even slower return journey now that Amelia had sole charge of their progress. They were right. Immersed in her new passion to the point of obsession, The Writer wrote, sketched, measured, and wandered her way into every temple, round every statue and through every tomb from Aswan to Cairo. By the time they arrived back in the capital at the end of April she had overrun Murray's schedule by a full six weeks.

But she had found her vocation.

In 1880 Murray's published a revised edition of their *Handbook*. A small paragraph tucked away at the bottom of page 543 described the rock chamber 'discovered in 1874 by Miss A.B. Edwards the authoress and Mr A. MacCallum the artist'. By then the book of The Writer's journey, *A*

Thousand Miles up the Nile, was heading for its second very successful edition and The Writer herself had built up an enviable reputation as an Egyptologist. She devoted the rest of her life to writing and lecturing on the need to protect the treasures of the Nile from the depredations of historians, collectors, tourists and vandals alike and in 1882 was one of the founders of the London-based Egypt Exploration Fund, a public society for the organisation and funding of archaeological research.

On their return from Egypt in 1874, she and the faithful 'L' had set up house together in the West Country, and apart from the occasional lecture tour to Europe or America, that remained their home for eighteen years. They died within a few months of each other in 1892, when Amelia was sixty-one. True to her passion to the end, The Writer turned Internationally Renowned Archaeological Historian left the bulk of her estate to University College London for the establishment of the first English Chair of Egyptology.

When the great temples of Abu Simbel were moved, piece by laborious piece, to their new site in the 1960s, Amelia's rock chamber was not considered sufficiently important to warrant the same treatment. It now lies buried in a deep accumulation of silt under the waters of Lake Nasser.

CHAPTER FOUR

'HIGHLY RESPECTED MISS KATE'
· Kate Marsden ·

 n a freezing February morning in 1891, the Chief of Police of the small town of Zlatoust was driven into the station yard. Alighting from the municipal sledge, he was greeted by a Colonel of the Police Mounted Division, twenty of whose men were lined up smartly at the entrance to the platform in a guard of honour. At the Colonel's orders the small crowd of curious villagers who had braved the icy wind were herded back to a respectful distance – the train from Moscow was coming; the honoured guests were about to arrive and their progress must not be impeded in any way.

With much rumbling and hissing and belching of steam, the huge engine slowed to a stop. The squad of mounted police snapped to attention, the station master straightened his collar, the crowd peered and craned their necks, a porter leapt to open the carriage door and the anxiously awaited visitors stepped down onto the snow-covered platform.

If their appearance caused the Police Chief some amusement, he allowed no trace of this to show. The first visitor handed him a sheet of paper, he read it carefully, handed it back with a low bow and turned to accompany them out to their waiting transport. The crowd were less deferential – as the official party emerged from the station several faces looked distinctly surprised, others grinned, while the children pointed and stared.

The Police Chief was furious. These were no ordinary travellers – they carried a letter of introduction from none other than Her Majesty the Empress Marie Fedorovna herself, together with instructions to whomever it may concern that they were to be given every assistance. The people of Zlatoust should be ashamed of showing so little respect.

Had he but known it, the stouter of the two dignitaries at his side had every sympathy with the crowd, and did not blame them in the least for grinning. She knew she looked ridiculous; she hated looking ridiculous; and there was not a single thing she could do about it.

It is not surprising that they stared for I was broadened and lengthened by so many inches I had failed to recognise myself in the looking glass. I had on a whole outfit of warm undergarments, then a loose kind of body lined with flannel, a very thickly wadded eiderdown ulster with sleeves long enough to cover the hands entirely, the fur collar reaching high enough to cover the head and face. Then a sheepskin reaching to the feet and furnished with a collar to come over the fur one. Then over the sheepskin I had to wear a *dacha*, which is a fur coat made of reindeer skin. And even now I have not come to the end of the list. I wore a long pair of stockings made of long hair, over them a pair of gentleman's thickest hunting stockings, over them a pair of Russian boots made of felt coming high up over the knee and over them a pair of brown felt *valenkies*. All this immense load of wool and fur and skins to cover a bit of frail and feeble humanity – yet there was not an ounce too much, as after-experience showed.

The 'bit of frail and feeble humanity' inside this shapeless bundle was Miss Kate Marsden; her companion, similarly accoutred, was Miss Ada Field, a shadowy figure reminiscent of Amelia Edwards's nameless friend 'L', and they were on their way to Siberia.

More specifically they were on their way from Moscow to the Yakutsk province of Eastern Siberia – as the crow flies, a distance almost exactly as great as that from London to Bombay or from New York to Rio de Janeiro. It was Miss Marsden's first visit to Russia, she spoke not a single word of the language when she set out, would speak very little more when she returned eleven months later, and for more than three-quarters of her journey she would travel without a companion. Yet as far as she was concerned Yakutsk would only be the starting point.

By describing herself as a 'bit of frail and feeble humanity' Kate was, luckily, speaking metaphorically. Although she was sparing with personal details when she wrote about her travels, she does make coy reference on more than one occasion to her fragility or her helplessness. There could have been just a touch of wishful thinking in this – although she would have been horrified to think anyone could suspect her of anything so frivolous. More probably it was a rather sad attempt to enlist the sympathy of her readers who, she imagined, would more readily identify with the problems facing a weak and defenceless female than with those overcome by a strong and very capable one. For in fact the thirty-one-year-old Kate was a tall, angular, plain-featured woman, possessed of a great deal of common sense and quite remarkable stamina.

Needless to say she was not, like Amelia Edwards, travelling for pleasure. Neither was she forced into it by the need to earn her living, like Anna Leonowens. She was travelling through Russia, as Emily Eden had travelled through India, because it was her duty to do so. But whereas Emily's sense of duty had been born of a mixture of affection, convention and family loyalty, Kate's was something different. Hers was a God-given, obsessional sense of duty – a crusade almost. She was going to Siberia to look for lepers.

★   ★   ★   ★

The plight of lepers throughout the world had been brought sharply to public attention by the death two years before, in 1889, of the Belgian priest, Father Damien. His work amongst the lepers on the Hawaiian island of Molokai, and his voluntary incarceration for life in their midst, had led finally to his contracting and dying from their dreadful disease. The future King Edward VII, then Prince of Wales, was moved to write of his extraordinary work and sacrifice: 'The heroic life and death of Father Damien has not only aroused the sympathy of the United Kingdom, but it has gone deeper – it has brought home to us that the circumstances of our vast Indian and Colonial Empire, oblige us, in a measure at least, to follow his example.'

As a result of this royal tribute, leprosy had become something of a fashionable cause amongst the charitable ladies of the English middle classes. But although Kate Marsden was both English and middle-class she was not tempted to join in with their discussion groups, sewing bees and fund-raising bazaars. She had something more positive to offer; she was a qualified and experienced nurse already familiar with the gruesome horror of leprosy.

The daughter of a London solicitor, Kate had been born in 1859, just four years after Florence Nightingale had brought the nursing profession into respectability during the Crimean War. The death of her mother when Kate was eleven sent her hitherto successful father into an emotional and professional decline. His practice suffered and the family's prosperity gradually diminished: when he died five years later Kate and her brothers and sisters were left with no option but to fend for themselves. She started her nursing training at the strongly Evangelical Tottenham Hospital in the London suburb of Edmonton where the sisters in charge were impressed with her 'decided nursing talent and ability'. After only eight months training she was sent with a group of fellow nurses to Bulgaria to tend Russian soldiers wounded in the Russo–Turkish war. It was here, when she was just eighteen years old, that she first came into contact with lepers.

> My acquaintance with the ravages of the frightful disease, and the sight of the poor, mutilated and helpless Bulgarians, aroused emotions in me that cannot fully be described. Who cared for them? What medical attention did they receive? What tender ministrations from the gentle hand of woman soothed

their sufferings? Cut off from their fellow-creatures, avoided, despised, and doomed to a living death with no remedy and no relief – surely these of all afflicted people demand, in a special and unique manner, human aid.

More than ten years would pass between her first contact with lepers and her decision to devote herself to their cause. On her return from the Balkans she had continued her medical training at the Westminster Hospital and spent four years in charge of a convalescent home in Liverpool. In 1884 she had travelled to New Zealand to care for her sister who was gravely ill with tuberculosis. Despite Kate's loving care her sister had died, but Kate stayed on in New Zealand, taking up an appointment as Lady Superintendent of the Wellington Hospital, helping to set up the first New Zealand branch of the St John's Ambulance Brigade and delivering a series of lectures on hygiene and first-aid. It was there that she heard of the death of Father Damien.

Kate was a true Victorian spinster. Her strict Protestant upbringing had taught her that pleasure would have little part to play in the life she was expected to lead; charity and philanthropy were immutable obligations, and thanks or gratitude for any good that she happened to do were due entirely to the Almighty. A devout Christian by conviction as well as by education, she had at one time contemplated entering the church as a nun. Father Damien's story showed her another way forward. Suddenly the whole chain of events was clear; her nursing, her contact with the lepers in Bulgaria, her administrative experience at the Wellington Hospital and with the St John's Ambulance Brigade – these were not isolated, unconnected incidents, they were part of a divine plan. 'The conviction took hold of me that my mission in life was to minister to those who received the smallest attention and care of all God's creatures.'

She immediately applied to the Hawaiian government for permission to go and work in Father Damien's leper colony on Molokai. But the publicity that had followed his death had ensured that there were already more than enough volunteers, and in any case the Sisters of the Sacred Heart had taken over the running of the colony; Kate was turned down. So, with the Prince of Wales's words ringing in her ears, she returned to England with the intention of concentrating on the lepers of British India.

Her arrival in London from New Zealand, however, coincided with the arrival in London from Russia of an invitation that gave her thoughts yet another new direction. The Russian Red Cross Society wanted to present her with a medal in recognition of her services during the Russo–Turkish war, and she was invited to go to Moscow for the presentation. It was easy for one of Kate's faith and enthusiasm to discern the hand of God in this diversion. She accepted the invitation and immediately set about arming herself to do battle on behalf of the lepers of the Russian Empire.

With a temerity that she thought must be divinely inspired since it certainly did not come naturally, she made a direct appeal to the Princess of Wales for patronage and was rewarded with a personal letter of introduction to the Empress of Russia. But when word of her impending mission reached the worthy ladies at their sewing bees they bristled indignantly. Determined not to let their own charitable efforts be upstaged by Miss Marsden's more ambitious plans, they were soon sharpening their tongues and their pencils as assiduously as they had previously plied their needles. Kate found herself accused of being a melodramatic publicity-seeker, of ignoring the popular stricture that 'charity begins at home' and of heading for Russia on a 'pleasure trip'.

The first of these charges was easy to deal with; of course she was seeking publicity – how else could she hope to raise the necessary funds and support for her mission? Likewise the second charge – certainly there was disease and suffering in England, but there were also churches and hospitals and philanthropic organisations within easy reach of the poor and the sick. She intended to devote herself to the plight of those for whom no such relief was available.

The third charge, however, struck her as so unjust that she could not resist a sharp retort – and a challenge – to her accusers.

> I may be called an enthusiast, or a woman who bids high for the world's applause. I care not what I am called or what I am thought of so long as the goal of my ambition be reached. Some people have said that I am going to take a 'pleasure trip'. So let it be. I plead guilty to the accusation on the one condition that all ladies who give this seductive term to my journey will agree to undertake an identical journey themselves.

Before leaving for Moscow Kate determined to find out everything she could about leprosy, current methods for treating the disease – if any such existed – and the conditions in which those lepers who received no treatment were forced to live. Such evidence as she could find was often conflicting. In some parts of the world there were said to be well-equipped leper hospitals staffed by qualified medical personnel. In other places not only were there no such facilities, but lepers were shamefully neglected and sometimes even actively persecuted by their communities. In the face of such contradictory evidence Kate realised the only thing to do was go and see for herself, 'taking no report at second hand'.

Travelling across the Black Sea and the Caucasus she arrived in Moscow in November 1890. 'Anyone who has been travelling through a strange country for three days and nights without stopping and ignorant of the language of the natives will easily understand my feelings of relief. . . especially if my reader is tall, and has experienced that awkward position of being cramped for a long period in a railway carriage.' The startling cold that pierced her English winter woollies; the quaint narrow streets; the ubiquitous horse-sledges moving so silently across the snow that their drivers constantly had to shout to warn of their approach; the crowds of people so muffled in furs that it was surprising they could either see the sledges or hear the shouts; the myriad gold-domed churches with white walls picked out in green or blue or lavender; all these new and wonderful sights distracted her attention for a whole afternoon. But then it was down to work.

As soon as she had been presented with her medal she asked her new-found friends at the Red Cross for the appropriate introductions. They directed her towards the Governor of Moscow, Prince Dolgorukov, who agreed to grant her an audience.

> The etiquette at such audiences is to appear in full day dress. Happily I had my nurse's uniform with me, which suits all occasions. So I brushed it up and, with a clean pair of strings to my somewhat worn bonnet, I concluded my toilette and finally set off, not without a feeling of nervousness, which unfortunately I can seldom shake off. Arriving at the palace I was soon ushered into the presence of the Prince, who, by his kind manner and gentle voice, at once banished every uncomfortable feeling. I told him about my mission and asked his permission to visit the hospitals of the city and any lepers to be found in it.

The Prince was more than helpful. He summoned the Inspector of Hospitals and ordered him to facilitate Kate's mission in any way he could. At this stage Kate had probably never even heard of Yakutsk – certainly Siberia was not on her itinerary. The Prince's ready co-operation therefore suddenly made her task appear quite simple. But that would all change when she presented her letter of introduction and outlined her plans to Her Majesty the Empress. Twice over the following few weeks Kate made the twelve-hour journey to St Petersburg where the Empress 'entered with readiness and sympathy into my philanthropic proposals', and confirmed the report Kate had heard both in Constantinople and in Tiflis (Tbilisi) of the existence of a herb which was said to alleviate the sufferings caused by leprosy. The only problem, as Marie Fedorovna saw it, was that the herb was rumoured to be found only in the far-off province of Yakutsk in Eastern Siberia, where, by chance, there were also thought to be a substantial number of lepers.

Nothing could have been clearer to Kate. First the Almighty had brought her to Russia and now He had shown her exactly where her task lay.

She would go to Siberia. She would find out all she could about the lepers and she would track down the magical herb and bring it back to Moscow.

In Moscow, as in London, there were those who questioned the wisdom and value of Kate's mission. Indeed her resolve to set off on such an extraordinary journey led some to suspect her of being a political spy – 'no laughing matter', she admonished any reader who might find something funny in the idea. But there were also plenty of charitable ladies ready to sponsor her efforts with money, provisions and advice; particularly when it became known that the Tsaritsa had given her personal blessing to the venture.

> When we came to consider such matters as stores and outfits there was quite a titillation of excitement; and even my own attention, I must confess, was diverted from the lepers for a moment in thinking what to wear and what provisions to take. Everyone was eager to suggest something in the way of food that combined keeping qualities with tastiness. Consequently, tinned and potted meats and fish, and bottled fruits and so on were mentioned in wondrous variety. But after all it was decided that we need only take a few boxes of sardines, biscuits, some bread, tea and one or two other trifles, which included forty pounds of plum pudding! This delicious compound would certainly 'keep' in cold weather, as all housewives know, and I liked it so was persuaded to take it as the staple article of the journey. I am afraid, however, that I frequently irritated my friends when, in the midst of discussing these things, I went off at a tangent to speak of the far-off lepers, and what they wanted.

Letters of introduction were obtained to influential persons in Siberia, stores were bought, clothes made, and in a few weeks everything was ready for 'this perilous, long and unknown journey'. Since it was out of the question for a respectable spinster to set out on such a journey alone, Kate had been forced to find a suitable female companion. Miss Ada Field qualified on two counts – firstly, unlike Kate, she could speak Russian, and secondly she was too timid to argue with her determined friend. Thus it was that the two ladies found themselves and their plum puddings being escorted from the train by the Chief of Police in Zlatoust. 'The honour accorded was, of course, to her Majesty and not to me.'

*   *   *   *

Had she waited for another ten years before launching herself into the wilds, Kate's journey would have been infinitely easier. Plans to build a Trans-Siberian railway had been agreed in principle in 1885, but the building of the first 2000-mile section, from the Ural mountains to Irkutsk on the shores of Lake Baikal, would not get under way until six months after Kate set out. Although construction of the railway would start simultaneously at five different points along the proposed line, this main section would not be opened until 1898 and the final link to the Pacific coast not until 1916. In February 1891, though, the line from Moscow ended at Zlatoust, at the foot of the Ural mountains.

Although technically they would reach Siberia as soon as they crossed the Urals, the Yakutsk province which was their destination still lay more than 3000 miles ahead. About their crossing of the Urals Kate would say little – probably because she was too dazed to notice much. Anxious, though, to correct any picture her readers may have had of her gliding along country lanes tucked cosily into a picturesque Christmas-card sleigh, she informed them in no uncertain terms that a sledge-journey across Russia had nothing whatsoever to do with gliding and even less to do with either cosiness or comfort.

Long-distance travelling sledges were shaped like flattened coal-scuttles. They were unpadded and unsprung and had no seats. The wooden chests containing clothes and provisions were packed into the 'hold', and covered with a layer of straw. The passengers then sat, or reclined, on top of the straw, wedged themselves firmly into position, and covered themselves with blankets and furs; 'the compulsory nature of this reclining is apt to become rather trying to one of independent spirit, especially since you have no firm hold against which to brace your feet.' Although the covered end of the sledge protected them from behind, the open front acted like a scoop; Kate's horses had an unfortunate habit of 'dashing at full gallop through freshly formed snowdrifts', and not infrequently the ladies would disappear under an overblanket of snow which 'had a way of settling down the collars of our coats, melting, and then trickling down our necks, or even flying up our sleeves'.

This would all have been trying enough had the roads been level. As it was the roads – if roads they truly were – were broken, rutted, and littered with potholes; 'the driver actually had to pull up now and then and dismount, in order to see how deep the next hole was.'

Bump, jolt, bump, jolt – over huge frozen lumps of snow and into holes and up and down those dreadful waves and furrows. First you bump your head against the top, then the conveyance gives a lurch and you get an unexpected knock against the side; then you cross one of the ruts and, first, you are thrown violently forward against the driver and, second, you just as quickly rebound. This sort of motion is all very well for a few miles, but after a time it gets too monotonously trying. You ache from head to foot, you are bruised all over; your poor brain throbs until you give way to a kind of hysterical outcry, your headgear gets displaced and your temper, naturally, becomes slightly ruffled. At the end of the day you are dragged, in a semi-comatose state, from the sledge;

and on gaining a foothold you feel more like a battered old log of mahogany than a gently-nurtured Englishwoman.

Travelling at breakneck speed, at the mercy of drivers whom Kate described as 'tipsy Jehus forever sipping their beloved vodka', the two ladies bounced and lurched their way eastwards. They travelled through villages and forests, over frozen lakes and across rivers made doubly treacherous by the first signs of the spring thaw. At Ekaterinberg they stayed at 'an excellent American hotel' and visited the 'badly ventilated, badly lighted and badly kept' prison. At Tjumen they were entertained by the agent of the British and Foreign Bible Society and wondered, on leaving, whether they would ever see another English face.

Between these rare havens of comfort the only accommodation on offer was in the wayside 'post houses' set at intervals along the road. These were small, sturdy log-cabins which operated strictly on a first-come first-served basis, although there seemed to be no upper limit to the numbers allowed in. There were no staff, no service of any kind, and no furniture; just large stoves on which you could prepare your own meals from your own provisions, large quantities of 'moving specks of different sizes and families' wandering about the walls, and a pile of verminous sheepskins and rugs in the middle of the floor from which you could select the wherewithal to make a bed.

> The heat of these premises is grateful and comforting at first; but the state of the atmosphere in the morning, after a number of people enveloped in dirty sheepskins have been enjoying repose in a room without a chink of ventilation, is best left to the imagination. Some hours before dawn you long for the intense cold outside and you register a vow that never again as long as you live will you enter such a stifling hole. But alas for human constancy! The very next night, and perhaps for many nights, you will eagerly seek the shelter of one of these warm structures and sleep soundly until wakened by a sensation of approaching suffocation.

By the time they reached the town of Omsk, 600 miles into their journey, both ladies 'would have been considered, under ordinary circumstances, fit objects for a doctor's attention'. Luckily word of their impending arrival had preceded them and they were welcomed by the Governor with an invitation to stay in his house; 'cheerful news – certainly we were in no way reluctant to renew our acquaintance with feather beds and the comforts of the family circle.'

Two weeks of these home comforts were enough to restore Miss Marsden to vigorous health. But poor Miss Field was less resilient. Not all Kate's entreaties could persuade her to go a step further; she had had enough, she was too ill, she would have to return to Moscow.

Although she regretted her friend's ill health and her departure, the proprieties that Kate had deemed it so essential to observe in Moscow now seemed quite irrelevant. It never occurred to her to abandon her mission through lack of a suitable companion, and had it not been for the fact that she still spoke not a single word of Russian, she would have been quite happy to proceed on her own. But the Governor of Omsk, anxious to comply with the Imperial order that Kate should receive all the help she needed, refused to countenance such a plan. Indeed, so horrified had he been to hear how her life had been put at risk by 'tipsy' drivers overturning the sledge into snowdrifts on no less than seven occasions, that he decided someone 'more efficient than a common soldier' was needed to protect her. When she left Omsk at the end of March Kate was therefore escorted by one of the Governor's attachés, 'an old soldier who could speak French and a little English and, being also thoroughly well versed in his own language, all fears of future emergencies disappeared.'

*　　　*　　　*　　　*

By now Kate had been on the road for two months. Although the pace of her journey was much what she had been led to expect, she was bursting with zeal and good will towards her less fortunate fellow men and was becoming distinctly frustrated by the lack of opportunity to express them. Since there were, as yet, no lepers to succour, she turned her attention to another group of unfortunates who were well represented in the area – prisoners.

Following her first prison visit in Ekaterinberg, she had made a point of asking permission to see the prisons in every town she passed through. Some, like the first, had been shocking in their wretchedness. Others, where there was a particularly enlightened Governor or an 'active community of true Christians', had been better built and better equipped. But in all of them she had been horrified to see the frightened, despairing looks on the faces of the shivering inmates and to hear the haunting rattle of the chains with which they were bound from waist to ankle.

She estimated that there were 40 000 prisoners from all corners of the Russian Empire incarcerated in Siberian gaols or on the move from one labour camp to another at the time she made her journey. Now, whenever word reached her that one of these groups was in the vicinity, she would set out to visit them armed with little parcels of tea and sugar for the refreshment of their bodies and sheaves of Gospels for the comfort of their souls.

I never could go to them clad in furs from head to foot when they were only scantily clothed and every blast of wind pierced through and through them. So I took some of my furs off; stuffed the large pockets of my ulster with tea and sugar, and with two bags strapped over my shoulders, I went into the midst of the gang. As my bare hands become numbed from exposure to the cold, and the icy wind went through me, I realised in some trifling measure the same physical suffering which they were enduring. I gave a double quantities to the women, who sometimes were nursing their babies. To see their grateful looks as I put the packets of tea and sugar and a Testament into their hands was worth all the trials that I had suffered and all that were to come.

The convicts provided Kate with a perfect interim cause to which to devote herself. The satisfaction of knowing she was being useful put her in the best of moods, and the 800 miles to Tomsk were accomplished without a hitch. It was now late April, and although the nights could still be frosty, much of the snow had melted. After the next 500-mile stage to Krasnoyarsk she would have to swap her sledge for a *tarantass*, according to the OED 'a four-wheeled Russian travelling carriage without springs on a flexible wooden chassis'; according to Kate Marsden 'an abominable construction in which a day's travel leaves you in need of a month's rest'.

One thousand miles over ruts and potholes in this unspeakable vehicle was enough to reduce even the sturdy Miss Marsden to a quivering wreck. But at least it covered the ground more quickly than the sledge and she reached the town of Irkutsk in the middle of May. Now she really was nearing her goal. Irkutsk was the administrative capital of central Siberia and it was here that she would find the doctors, churchmen and officials who could provide her with all the available information about the lepers she had come so far to help.

After two days rest I called on the Governor-General who received me with great kindness and corroborated all I had heard about the state of the Yakutsk lepers. I suggested the formation of a committee of influential people in Irkutsk who could arouse the sympathy and obtain the help of the merchants of the town on behalf of their poor lost brethren in the north. His Excellency graciously agreed to this proposal and, in order that I might be fully prepared for it, he furnished me with an official statement regarding the current position of the lepers.

Reading the statement, Kate discovered that there were said to be eighty lepers in the region of Yakutsk, but that it was supposed that there were far more, as the Yakuts did everything in their power to disguise their infection for fear of being expelled from the community, the inevitable fate of every leper. The causes of the disease were thought to be the primitive living conditions of the Yakuts, the immense forests, the endless marshes, the dampness of the air, the unclean habits of the 'natives', their food of rotten fish, water taken from the marshes and lakes, the insufficiency of bread, meat, salt and other essential nutrients in their diet and the frequent famines that assailed the country. Although a small hospital had been built to house forty lepers in the Sredni Viluisk region in 1860, owing to the insufficiency of means it had been closed three years later. Since then there had been no possibility of assigning more funds for a special shelter for lepers.

The gloomy picture painted by this report convinced Kate, if indeed she had ever doubted, that her work was vital. This knowledge gave her the confidence to address, through an interpreter, a full working committee meeting of all the notables of Irkutsk, a meeting at which she was treated 'with the utmost kindness and courtesy by all present, each trying to surpass the other in politeness and kind attention. They promised to carry out every suggestion and bound themselves to help in every way in their power.' The meeting ended with Kate being appointed official investigator on behalf of the Irkutsk authorities with the specific task of finding out exactly how many lepers there were in the Viluisk region, reporting on the conditions in which they lived, and making recommendations as to the best way of alleviating their suffering.

She was jubilant. Those were exactly the things she had come to do. Now she had not only Imperial support but official authorisation – surely she could not fail. Leaping with renewed vigour into her *tarantass*, she set off on the last stage of the journey to Yakutsk.

> 150 miles brought us to the River Lena, where we were to resume the journey by water. The barge which carried us was little better than a raft intended for transporting goods between Irkutsk and Yakutsk. I had to sleep amongst the cargo and for the three weeks which the journey occupied we had to rough it in every way.

Refraining, for fear of boring her readers, from enumerating the many inconveniences and troubles which she had to bear on the barge, 'and which alone might have filled a volume', Kate restricted herself to thanking God for sparing her life for long enough to reach her goal. She stepped ashore in the town of Yakutsk in the middle of June 1891.

*　　*　　*　　*

Eastern Siberia is a region that experiences greater extremes of climate than anywhere else in the world. From a record winter low of −90°F the temperature can soar in summer to as much as 100°F. The province of Yakutsk extends over two and a half million square miles – an area larger than the whole of France – and, at the end of the nineteenth century, had a population of less than 100 000. It is a vast wilderness of forests, marshes and lakes and although there was one road marked on the map Kate was given, she soon discovered that it was a road that existed 'only in the imagination of the mapmaker'.

She did not think much of the town of Yakutsk, 'not a pretty place, with a dead and dreary appearance', but she had no complaints about the warmth of her welcome. The local dignitaries turned out in force to greet her and the Bishop promised to do everything in his power to expedite her mission. To Kate's delight he also confirmed the existence of the herb she had resolved to find.

> On my referring to the herb he said, much to my surprise, that he had a few specimens, and before I left he placed some in my hands. He could give no definite information as to its curative or alleviating properties, but it was a source of some satisfaction that the reports I had heard were not altogether groundless.

Her second stroke of good fortune in Yakutsk was her meeting with Jean Procopieff. This gentleman, an elderly Cossack, was so impressed by Kate's endeavours on behalf of the lepers that he not only offered to lend her both men and horses for the next stage of her journey, but also volunteered his services as 'leader of the cavalcade' at least as far as Viluisk. She was delighted to accept.

'Our cavalcade was a curious one. It consisted of fifteen men, thirty horses, and myself.' The escort, she explained, was essential not only because there were so many stores to be carried but also as a means of protection against 'the dangers to be encountered, not the least amongst them being the bears, with which the woods are infested'.

There was obviously no point in trying to travel any further in a *tarantass*, 'such a conveyance would have got wedged fatally in the forest or would have sunk in some treacherous morass before a single mile had been covered.' So now, if she was to reach the pathetic, outcast groups of lepers cowering in the forests, she would have to adapt herself to a third new form of transport – horseback. But the roughness of the terrain and the notorious intractability of the Yakutsk horses made it impossible for her to ride on a side-saddle, even had such a contraption been available in Siberia. It therefore followed that she would have to adopt 'man's mode' of riding and, consequently, 'man's mode' of dress – a circumstance that caused her a good deal of embarrassment.

> I was obliged to ride as a man for several reasons – first because the Yakutsk horses were so wild that it was impossible to ride sideways; second because no woman could ride on a lady's saddle for three thousand versts; third because in

the absence of roads the horse has a nasty propensity for stumbling on the stones and amongst the roots of trees, which in these virgin forests make a perfect network, thus precipitating the unfortunate rider on to the ground; and fourth because the horse frequently sinks into the mud up to the rider's feet, and then, recovering its footing, rushes madly amongst the shrubs and branches, utterly regardless of the fact that the lady-rider's dress (if she wore one) was being torn into shreds. For these reasons I think no one will blame me for making adequate provisions against the probability of bruises, contusions etc. I rather shrink from giving a description of my costume, because it was so inelegant.

In fact the trousers, jacket, deer-stalker and thick leather boots probably suited her rather well. Certainly they made the next stage of her journey if not comfortable, at least practicable. She also carried a revolver in case she should be attacked by bears, but since she had no idea how to fire it, she handed it to one of her escort in case she shot a man by mistake.

If Kate had found the journey to Yakutsk something of an ordeal, she would soon be looking back on it as simplicity itself. Not only had she seldom ridden a horse before, but she had never ridden astride and had never encountered anything quite so uncomfortable as her broad, bare and extremely hard wooden saddle. Now she found herself spending up to twelve hours a day sitting on this instrument of torture, travelling through trackless marshes and dense, prickly forests. The intense heat of the sun and the frequent drenching rainstorms meant that she was alternately stifled and dripping wet. She dared not let go of the reins for fear of her horse bolting and was therefore unable to brush off the clouds of mosquitoes and flies that swarmed around them every moment of the day and night, penetrating every crevice in her clothing and bringing her hands, wrists and face up in great swollen weals.

At the end of each day's ride she was so exhausted that she had to be lifted out of the saddle, and then she very often just lay down and fell fast asleep on the spot without having anything to eat. And yet, even at the worst moments, when she was moved to wonder whether she would not be better off dead, she knew that there was nowhere else on earth that she would rather be.

Two weeks and 250 miles north-west from Yakutsk they at last reached the Viluisk region where there were known to be lepers. The following day the local priest took Kate to the site of the hospital that had been built in 1860 and closed from lack of funds in 1863. There was nothing left except a few stumps in the ground to mark where it had stood. The Yakuts who accompanied them would not even approach the site, so great was their terror of the disease. The priest then led Kate into the surrounding forest.

At last I thought I could discern ahead a lake and beyond that two huts. My instinct was true to me; and the peculiar thrill which passed through my whole frame meant that, at last, after all these months of travelling, I had found, thank God, the poor creatures whom I had come to help. A little more zigzag riding along the tedious path and then I suddenly looked up and saw before me the two huts and a little crowd of people. Some of them came limping, and some leaning on sticks, to catch the first glimpse of us, their faces and limbs distorted by the dreadful ravages of the disease. One poor creature could only crawl by the help of a stool and all had the same indescribably hopeless expression of the eyes. I scrambled off the horse and went quickly amongst them.

The stories Kate would have to tell about the sufferings of these abandoned 'scraps of humanity' make harrowing reading. The moment any person was even suspected of having leprosy he or she was literally driven out of the community and thereafter not allowed to approach within two or three miles of any village. Such food as was left for them was invariably old and bad, such clothes as they were given mere rags. The Yakutsk Medical Inspector was unable to give her a full description of the *yourtas* in which they lived because however much he wanted to get acquainted with the interior of these huts, he 'could not get into them on account of the stench, similar to that coming from a dead body; which was due not only to the lepers themselves, but also to the food that they ate, consisting chiefly of rotten fish.' They received no medical attention at all either for their suppurating sores or for any other infections to which their debilitated physical condition left them such easy prey. Even spiritual assistance was denied to most of them, since none but the most selfless of priests dared do more than pay them an annual visit, bless the living from a safe distance and say a prayer over the graves of the dead as he hastened away.

In one village she was told of an orphan boy of six or seven years old, in whom leprosy was suspected but never confirmed, who had been taken by his uncle into the middle of one of the densest forests in the district and abandoned there with nothing but a rickety shelter of sticks and dried cow dung to protect him from the Siberian winter. 'Without food, without warmth, frightened by the sounds of wild creatures, shaking with cold, startled by the fierce winds howling in the trees, driven to the verge of madness, and with no possibility of finding his way back to his uncle's house, the terrified child had been left to die.'

Among the lepers in one of the settlements she came across an eighteen-year-old girl whose mother had developed the disease whilst pregnant: although the daughter had been born healthy and had never developed leprosy herself, her relatives would not allow her to return to her village and she had been forced to live her whole life as an outcast surrounded by the sick, the mutilated and the dying. It was a measure of Kate's influence that, at her urgent request, the local Police Inspector agreed to rescue this poor girl from her fate and employ her as a servant in his own home.

Although she had been expecting their conditions to be bad, Kate had had no inkling of how truly atrocious they would be. She visited three other settlements in the Sredni Viluisk region, each one worse than the last, and the horrors that met her eyes nearly made her faint. But anger kept her going, and a grim determination that every official she met, every priest, every soldier and every healthy peasant must be roused to action on behalf of the outcasts.

For a month she and her companions quartered the forests. It was now late July and the long hours of summer daylight allowed them to travel fifty or sixty miles a day. Their diet was limited to those few provisions which had survived such mishaps as bolting pack-horses and drenching thunder-storms – mostly 'dried bread almost as hard as stone which had to be soaked in tea before being eaten'. Inevitably the emotional and physical effort took its toll. One particularly gruelling expedition to reach a remote settlement involved a fifteen-mile ride, followed by a four-mile boat trip and then a ten-mile walk through the forest.

> Having been without sleep for twenty-four hours and not having broken my fast for twelve I was not exactly in good training for that pedestrian feat. On the way back I got on tolerably well for about three miles, and then simply dropped.

Her escort stepped in. Since they were under strict instructions to ensure that she came to no harm they ignored her protests that she would recover after a moment's rest and, between them, carried her back to the river. Once they had rowed her across they strapped her onto her horse and took her straight back to Viluisk. 'Then I went to bed and slept for twenty-four hours. That rest was indeed a godsend for we had to start in two days on a journey of six hundred miles.'

When they set out two days later they headed north-east. Now they were travelling towards Verkoyansk on the edge of the Arctic Circle. Although they had already tracked down eight separate groups of lepers, Kate knew there were more to find. But even the horrors she had already encountered had not prepared her for those that lay ahead.

> Halting at the leper settlement of Hatignach a scene met my eyes too horrible to describe fully. Twelve men, women and children, scantily and filthily clothed, were huddled together in two small huts covered with vermin. The stench was dreadful; one man was dying, two men had lost their toes and half their feet and they had tied boards from their knees to the ground so that they could drag themselves along. The fur of their tattered clothes stuck to their open, weeping

sores. Two of the children were naked, having no clothes at all, and with the exception of a few rags they are in the same state in winter. As I sat there among them, the flies were tormenting their festering wounds and some of them were writhing in agony. There were traces of bear here and I began to wonder why some of these lepers did not, in their desperation, throw themselves in the way of the bears and so end their miseries.

Almost as upsetting as their physical condition was the pathetic joy with which each group of lepers greeted her arrival. She had nothing to offer them except little packets of tea, an occasional blanket, the assurance that she would not let them be forgotten, and her prayers. Even these meagre scraps of comfort had them grovelling at her feet in gratitude, and Kate would find herself stumbling away from their forest clearings blinded by her own tears. In the face of their desolation the inadequacy of her efforts amplified their cries of thanks into haunting shrieks of pain. How could they thank her when in all probability most of them would have died long before any real relief could reach them?

By now it had become obvious to her that conditions would only improve if attitudes in the local communities changed. If there were special colonies like the one established by Father Damien on Molokai, properly equipped to meet their needs, those suspected of being infected need not be driven into the woods to live like animals. If they were no longer faced with that dreadful prospect, lepers in the early stages of the disease would be less tempted to try and disguise their condition and thus risk spreading infection through the community. Isolation would still be essential, but the lepers could live useful lives with dignity and comfort – the ghastly forest ghettos could become a thing of the past.

Throwing diplomacy to the winds, with her Bible in one hand and her letter from the Empress in the other, Kate marched into the homes, offices and churches of the leaders of every community she entered. She bossed, she remonstrated, she cajoled and she threatened – surely this or that mayor/priest/official did not want to be the only one in the whole of Yakutsk province to ignore an Imperial request? She knew they were intelligent, compassionate people who would understand and appreciate the situation. If they would form a committee to raise funds for such a colony she would consider it a great honour to be their patron, and she would be sure to mention their efforts in her report to Her Imperial Majesty in St Petersburg.

Almost without exception she found the people in authority to be well aware of the desperate conditions in which their lepers struggled to survive. But Viluisk was a remote, impoverished region of no special significance to such central authorities as could have provided the means to improve the situation. Over the years any efforts they had made had foundered from lack of organisation and, more frequently, from lack of funds, with the result that even the most philanthropic of officials had become sadly dispirited.

It was most gratifying for Kate to realise that it was this, as much as the letter from the Empress, that accounted for the enthusiasm with which she was welcomed by those she approached. The publicity that would be generated in Yakutsk, Irkutsk and even far-off Moscow and St Petersburg by her story seemed likely to do almost as much good (she would never presume to say 'more good' even if that, patently, was her aim) as all their prayers.

As great an obstacle as the lack of facilities was, however, the fear and ignorance of the 'natives' themselves. Although it was official policy (in so far as there was an official policy) to isolate the lepers, it was their own terror of becoming infected that caused the villagers to treat them with such mindless cruelty. Partly because she could not speak their language, and partly because she had so little time at her disposal, Kate admitted less success in tackling this aspect of the problem.

In one village she managed to persuade the inhabitants to provide the lepers in their district with a sledge and a horse so that they would not be forced to crawl the three miles from their huts to the point where food was sometimes left for them. In another she tried to explain that since these desperate creatures were nevertheless God's creatures, they surely deserved better provisions than the putrid fish and occasional bowl of rancid milk that was their present lot and on whose regular delivery they could not depend.

But her passion to convert others to her cause was leading her to dangerous neglect of her own health. By the middle of September she and her wild Yakuti horse had covered 2000 miles, during the course of which she had visited thirteen separate groups of lepers and had met and spoken to sixty-six men, women and children suffering from the disease. To achieve this she had struggled and floundered through countless marshes, she had survived forest fires, thunderstorms and 'bear-alarms' and several times her unruly mount had bolted with her through dense forests in the pitch dark. She had drunk 'abominably dirty water as only thirsty people can drink' and had slept in wet clothes for nights on end. She could do no more.

I have never experienced such utter exhaustion of both mind and body. My hands literally refused to hold the reins of my horse; there lay the reins; I knew they had to be held, but I was totally incapable of communicating any power to my hands. Added to this I was suffering acute pain from an interior abscess which the constant riding had formed. With my head as dull as a lump of lead I tied the reins round my wrist and let the horse do just as he liked. This sort of

Above: *Emily Eden from a painting by F. Rochard, 1835.*

Inset: *Ranjit Singh, the 'Lion of the Punjab', from a painting by Emily Eden.*

Top left: *The only known picture of Anna Leonowens.*
Bottom left: *King Mongkut of Siam with one of his favourite wives.*

Below: *One of the many princely pupils of Anna Leonowens, attended by a slave. Slavery was one of the practices in Siam to which Anna objected so strongly.*

Top left: *Amelia Edwards, who 'drifted to Egypt by accident'.*
Bottom left: *Amelia Edwards' sketch of the entrance to her rock chamber at Abu Simbel.*

Below: *Kate Marsden, about to set out from Yakutsk on the last leg of her journey to the leper settlements of Eastern Siberia.*
Bottom left and right: *Kate Marsden, 'a bit of frail and feeble humanity'.*

Inset: *Gertrude Bell as a young woman.*

Top: *Gertrude Bell beside an Arab funerary monument in 1900.*

Bottom: *Inside the tent of Muhammad Abu Tayyi, Sheikh of the Howeitat.*

Top: *Daisy Bates*, Kabbarli *(or dreamtime grandmother) to the aborigines*.

Bottom: *Daisy Bates giving medical assistance to one of her aborigine 'grandchildren'*.

Top: *Yongden, Alexandra David-Neel and a local child below the Potala Palace in Lhasa.*
Bottom: *Alexandra David-Neel on her second foray over the Tibetan border in 1915.*

equestrianship failed to please my escort so a cart was hired, a layer of hay placed at the bottom and I was placed on it. Thus I re-entered Yakutsk.

Her return journey took three months. At Irkutsk and Krasnoyarsk, Tomsk, Omsk and Ekaterinberg she summoned enough strength to call on those who had promised her their support and gave them an account of her experiences. She reported on the conditions she had found in Yakutsk and urged them to greater efforts on behalf of the lepers she had met. The intervening stages between these cities would never be more than a blur in her memory. There was the time when the horses pulling her *tarantass* took fright and bolted, jerking the driver forward out of his seat to be trampled to death under their thrashing feet; there was the night when she finally rebelled against the squalor of a post station only to find that the peasant couple who offered her alternative accommodation expected her to share a bed not just with them but also with the husband's two brothers. But mostly there was just jolting and lurching and cold and fleas and aching fatigue.

Faithful Miss Ada Field had driven out as far as Tjumen to welcome her friend home; 'the little life left in me was kept from expiring by her unceasing care and ever watchful consideration. How thankful I was to God that my former steadfast companion was at my side again.'

Kate arrived back in Moscow in December 1891, eleven months after setting out. She allowed herself just three days rest before leaving again for St Petersburg where she hoped to establish 'the headquarters of a scientific society for investigating the state of lepers, and controlling measures for their relief wherever lepers existed throughout the Russian Empire'.

*　　　*　　　*　　　*

She stayed in Russia for another six months, lecturing, fund-raising, discussing plans for the proposed Viluisk leper colony and being fêted by the 'philanthropic organisations' of both Moscow and St Petersburg. She was granted another audience with the Empress at which Her Majesty volunteered to head the list of donors to Kate's fund. By the time she left for England in May 1892 more than 25 000 roubles had been raised towards the establishment of the colony, and four nuns from a community of Sisters of Mercy in Moscow were already on their way to Yakutsk to take up Kate's work there. Her prayers were being answered. Her only sadness was that she had been unable to find any signs of the magical herb growing anywhere in Yakutsk and the samples she had been given had not survived the journey back to Moscow.

Just before her departure she was invited to attend the annual meeting of

the Moscow Dermatological Society as guest of honour. The Vice-President
addressed the assembled company.

> When a tourist undertakes a long journey, it is certainly to satisfy his own
> curiosity. But when a woman decides to visit a distant country, thousands of
> miles from her own land; when she willingly submits to all the inconveniences
> of the journey – to the severe cold of an almost savage country, to hunger and
> fatigue, her only recompense being the hope of alleviating the sufferings of the
> victims of that most terrible of diseases, leprosy – then not only does the journey
> of such a woman merit the sympathies of scientists and philanthropists, but the
> person herself inspires their respect and their admiration.

Although she was quick to attribute her success 'not to human instrument-
ality but to the direct guidance and help of God', Kate was human enough
to enjoy her celebrity in Moscow. But she seemed to know that her
reception back in England would be a little different. And indeed it was.
The Royal Geographical Society acknowledged her achievements by
appointing her one of their first lady Fellows, and Queen Victoria herself
presented Kate with a gold brooch as a mark of her appreciation. Yet even
the inclusion in her book of more than thirty pages of signed testimonials
from pretty well every priest, princess, medical inspector, soldier or nun
that she encountered on her journey seemed unable to convince her critics
that she had accomplished anything of value on her 'pleasure trip'. In 1921
she was still apparently fighting her critics, this time by publishing *A
Vindication of My Mission to Siberia*. But even that did not seem to work.

In 1897 a leper colony was opened in Viluisk. It had ten separate houses
for lepers, two hospitals, a doctor, a laboratory, a church and a library – all
just as Kate had planned. She should have been triumphant. Instead she was
slumped into a depression from which she would never fully recover.
Nothing could ever be as rewarding and fulfilling as her 12 000-mile
journey through Russia; but in the course of it she had ruined her health and
would now never be fit enough to undertake another. She died in London in
1931.

CHAPTER FIVE

'BAPTISED OF THE DESERT'
· *Gertrude Bell* ·

sk six different people the question, 'Who was Gertrude Bell?' and the chances are you will receive six different replies. By some she is remembered as a poet, by others as a mountaineer. Some recall her as an archaeologist or a historian, some as a diplomat or a stateswoman, and yet others as the traveller who trailed her *haute couture* wardrobe across the Arabian deserts.

Even among her contemporaries opinions varied so widely that it is hard to believe their comments applied to one and the same person. 'A masterful woman who has everyone under her thumb,' wrote Virginia Woolf. 'A silly, chattering windbag' and 'a blethering ass', inveighed Mark Sykes, a fellow traveller and diplomat. But her stepmother believed that the real basis of Gertrude's nature was 'her capacity for deep emotion. Her ardent and magnetic personality drew the lives of others into hers as she passed along.'

At the height of her career Gertrude Bell was acknowledged to be the most powerful woman in the Middle East. Her long acquaintance with the peoples and lands of Asia Minor, Syria and Mesopotamia had culminated in her appointment to the post of Oriental Secretary to the British High Commissioner in the newly formed country of Iraq. She had been closely involved in the drawing-up of the frontiers of the post-First World War Middle East and her energetic endorsement of Faisal's claim to the Iraqi throne earned her the name 'Kingmaker'. In appreciation of her efforts on his behalf and in acknowledgement of her archaeological expertise, King Faisal subsequently appointed her Iraq's first Director of Antiquities and charged her with the founding of his country's National Museum.

'She was in her right place in Iraq,' wrote Vita Sackville-West, who visited her in Baghdad in 1926, 'in her own house, with her office in the city, and her white pony in a corner of the garden, and her Arab servants, and her English books, and Babylonian shards on the mantelpiece, and her long thin nose and irrepressible vitality. She had the gift of making you feel that . . . life was full and rich and exciting.'

But Vita, like many others before her, had been unable to penetrate Gertrude's emotional camouflage. Although she still managed to make others feel eager and optimistic, her own 'irrepressible vitality' was wearing out. Four months after Vita's visit, and two days before her own fifty-eighth birthday, Gertrude Bell died from an overdose of barbiturates.

In the manner of the times, the word 'suicide' was never mentioned publicly and as far as her father, step-mother and brother were concerned 'she died quite peacefully in her sleep'. But her death came as a devastating shock to everyone who had ever met her – it just did not seem possible that so much energy and talent, so much knowledge and so much enthusiasm could so suddenly cease to exist.

*   *   *   *

Gertrude Margaret Lowthian Bell was born in 1868, not only with a silver spoon in her mouth but with an embossed invitation in one hand, an encyclopaedia in the other and a magic carpet unrolled at her feet. The Bell family fortunes had been created by her grandfather Sir Isaac Lowthian Bell, iron-master and colliery owner extraordinary and founder of a thriving industrial empire in County Durham. His son Hugh, Gertrude's father, had inherited the best part of a million pounds from his hardworking and ambitious parent without having had to lift more than the occasional finger, but with the unwritten codicil that he use it to complete the family's rise into 'social respectability'.

Hugh Bell was faithful to his charge. Gertrude was brought up in the best traditions of the English gentry, in a large house where those 'below-stairs' outnumbered those 'above' by three to one, where nannies and nurserymaids and governesses held sway, where squads of gardeners kept the lawns like velvet and the flowerbeds were a year-round glory. Tragedy struck this elegant establishment while Gertrude was still too young to understand it; when she was three years old her mother died just a few days after giving birth to a son, Maurice, and for several years Hugh was devastated. But in 1877 he married again.

Florence Olliffe had grown up amongst the artistic and literary élite of Paris, and was connected either by blood, marriage or friendship to many of England's most prominent families. She brought to the Bell family all the culture, all the artistic imagination and all the 'social respectability' of which old Sir Isaac had dreamed; and she also brought great happiness to Hugh and to his children. Her relationship with her step-daughter was exemplary; from the very first Gertrude was happy to call Florence 'Mother'.

Until she was fifteen Gertrude was educated at home, where a succession of governesses struggled to interest her in such ladylike accomplishments as embroidery, cookery and piano-playing. But her aptitude for more scholarly pursuits had been obvious from an early age, and when her brother Maurice was sent away to Eton, Florence and Hugh decided that Gertrude too would benefit from a more formal education. In 1884 she went to London to stay with Florence's mother, Lady Olliffe, and to attend Queen's College in Harley Street. The history lecturer at Queen's College was so impressed with Gertrude's intelligence, and particularly with her aptitude for his subject, that towards the end of the second year he approached Hugh and Florence with a suggestion.

> He strongly urged us to let her go to Oxford and go in for the History School [wrote Florence]. The time had not yet come when it was a usual part of a girl's education to go to University, and it was with some qualms that we consented. But the result justified our decision. Gertrude went to Lady Margaret Hall in 1886 just before she was eighteen, she left it in June 1888 just before she was twenty, and wound up after those two years by taking a brilliant First Class in Modern History.

Although several paintings and photographs exist of Gertrude when she was a girl, they are mostly formal studio portraits. They show a striking face, with wide-set eyes and strong jaw, lacking perhaps only a touch of softness to turn the good looks into beauty; the determination is there and the self-assurance is unmistakeable. But it is from the recollections of her family and her friends, as well as from her own letters, that a far clearer picture emerges of her extraordinary energy and enthusiasm. Janet Hogarth, a friend and contemporary of Gertrude's at Oxford, remembered she 'took our hearts by storm with her brilliant talk, her youthful confidence in herself, her father and the vivid intellectual world in which she had been brought up. She was the most brilliant student we ever had at Lady Margaret Hall – the most alive at every point, with her tireless energy, her splendid vitality and her unlimited capacity for work, for talk and for play.'

It was in 1892, when Gertrude was twenty-four, that she had her first introduction to the Middle East. The new arrivals to Baghdad in the 1920s who were so overawed by her self-possession would have been reassured to know that her initial response to this strange world had been as wide-eyed and breathless as their own.

> How big the world is, how big and how wonderful. It comes to me as ridiculously presumptuous that I should dare to carry my little personality half across it and boldly attempt to measure with it things for which it has no table of measurements that can possibly apply.

Gertrude's stay in Teheran was just the first instance of Florence's countless relations being ideally placed to offer hospitality. On her travels in years to come she would find the doors of French and British embassies in almost every country she visited flung open to welcome her as soon as Florence's name was mentioned. This time it was Florence's sister Mary and her husband Frank Lascelles, the British Ambassador, who had invited Gertrude to visit them as part of an extended tour of European capitals. But Gertrude was very far from being the typical touring débutante. Already fluent in French and German, she had prepared for her visit to Teheran by spending the previous six months learning to read, write and speak Persian. Her reactions to the country illustrate a quality that Florence had recognised from an early age – 'she had a special gift of forming extremely rapid impressions of places and of people.'

> Here that which is me, which womanlike is an empty jar that the passer by fills at pleasure, is filled with such wine as in England I had never heard of. In this country the men wear flowing robes of green and white and brown, and the women lift the veil of a Raphael Madonna to look at you as you pass. Wherever there is water a luxuriant vegetation springs up, and where there is not there is nothing but stone and desert. Oh, the desert round Teheran! Miles and miles of it with nothing, *nothing* growing. I never knew what desert was till I came here; it is a very wonderful thing to see.

During the six months Gertrude spent in Persia with the Lascelles she continued her study of the language and joined in the diplomatic social whirl with her customary 'zest'. Almost inevitably, on this her first independent excursion from the confines of strictly conventional Victorian family life, she fell in love. Henry Cadogan was, on the face of it, not a bad choice; one of the secretaries to the British Legation, he was ten years older than Gertrude, handsome, charming, an excellent sportsman and with a love of history and literature that seemed to equal her own.

The romance flourished. For three months they saw each other almost every day; they went to parties and picnics, they played tennis and read poetry and went on long rides into the desert, and eventually Henry proposed. Hugh and Florence received an ecstatic letter from Gertrude asking for their permission to become engaged. They refused.

There was nothing wrong with Mr Cadogan's pedigree – he was, after all, the grandson of an earl – but they had heard some unfavourable rumours about his character. Not only was he an impecunious diplomat unlikely ever to rise to the top of his profession, but he was said to be a gambler who could not be relied upon to pay his debts. On no account would they permit

Gertrude to marry such a man, indeed they thought it better she return to England forthwith.

Although she tried hard to change their minds, it never occurred to Gertrude to rebel.

> Of course if Papa says it is out of the question there will be nothing for him to do but stay on in Persia for at least a year or more and for us both nothing but to wait until he is an Ambassador or something surprising and remunerative. . . . Some people live all their lives and never have this wonderful thing; at least I have known it and have seen life's possibilities suddenly open in front of me. Only one may cry just a little when one has to turn away and take up the old narrow life again.

By December 1892 she was back home in England – but she was spared the waiting. Nine months later Henry Cadogan fell from his horse into an icy river in southern Persia and died of pneumonia. Their nine-month separation had done nothing to alter Gertrude's feelings, and she mourned him deep and long. It would be twenty years before she fell in love again.

Gertrude's deference to her father's wishes, not entirely surprising in matters as weighty as her marriage, was nevertheless a remarkable feature of her behaviour throughout her life. Even as a successful career-woman in her forties she would, perhaps rhetorically, ask for his advice and his permission before undertaking any new venture. But if he was stern, Hugh Bell was not unsympathetic. When Gertrude arrived back in England he encouraged her to continue her studies in Persian and entirely approved of her expressed intention to see more of 'this immeasurable world'; indeed as often as possible he accompanied her.

With either Hugh or her brother Maurice for company, Gertrude spent much of the next seven years abroad. She visited France, Algeria, Germany and Greece; she pored over the art treasures of Italy and had her first experience of the newly fashionable sport of mountaineering in Switzerland. She stayed with the Lascelles again, but this time in Berlin where Frank was now Ambassador, and was introduced to Kaiser Wilhelm at a tea party. In 1897, as if finally to get the measure of it, she and Maurice travelled right round the world. Between trips she continued her Persian studies in London; 1894 saw the publication of her first book *Safar Nameh* – 'Persian Pictures', and in 1896 she completed her translation of the book of poetry that she had first read in Teheran with Henry Cadogan – the *Divan* of Hafiz. Florence noted that Gertrude was 'an ardent lover of poetry all her life, which was a strangely interesting ingredient in a character capable on occasion of very definite hardness, and of a deliberate disregard of sentiment; and also in a mental equipment which included great practical ability'. Her translation of the *Divan* was a perfect example of her using her 'mental equipment' in the cause of her love of poetry, and it earned her the admiration of some of the foremost Persian scholars of the day.

In October 1899 came her opportunity to return to the Middle East. While in Teheran she had become close friends with the German Consul-General Dr Rosen and his wife Nina, who was, inevitably, an old school friend of Florence's. Fritz Rosen was now German Consul-General in Jerusalem and Nina wrote inviting Gertrude to pay them an extended visit. She arrived in Jerusalem on 12 December 1899.

★ ★ ★ ★

The Rosens only had a small house and partly because she had no wish to impose upon them and partly, one suspects, because she preferred to be independent, Gertrude decided to stay in a small hotel just two minutes walk from the German Consulate. Her generous allowance from Hugh allowed her to live in some style: 'My apartment consists of a very nice bedroom and a big sitting room both opening onto a small vestibule which runs all along the first floor of the hotel. My housemaid is an obliging gentleman in a fez who brings me my hot bath in the morning and is ready at all times to fly around in my service.' Within twenty-four hours of her arrival she had arranged for an Arabic teacher to give her lessons and had bought herself a horse.

> My days are full and most agreeable, but I don't think I shall ever learn Arabic – there are five words for wall and 36 ways of forming the plural and the rest is like unto it. But I go on struggling with it in the hope of mortifying providence by my persistence. I now stammer a few words to my housemaid – him of the fez – and he is much delighted.

During the next six months she explored Jerusalem on foot and the surrounding countryside on horseback, and wrote a stream of letters home to her father, each one more enthusiastic than the last. With the Rosens she travelled east round the Dead Sea and then south to visit the ruins of Petra – an experience which inspired her to seven pages of eulogy to Hugh. She went north from Jerusalem towards the mountains of the Jebel Druse and then on across the plains to Damascus. When the Rosens' energy, enthusiasm or time ran out, she would wave them a cheery farewell and hurtle on without them, accompanied just by a cook and a few porters.

Clearly the fact that she was now thirty-one years old did not entirely ease her mind as to the propriety of her unaccompanied gallivanting; every now and then she would take time in her letters to apologise to Hugh for not having had his specific permission for this or that detour. But one of the fundamental joys of travelling abroad was the freedom it gave her from the strict rules which governed English society. This was particularly true of the Middle East where each man or woman, no matter how strange his behaviour, was merely considered to be following his own destiny. This tolerance, Gertrude argued, meant that it was wiser for a European not to seek to 'ingratiate himself with Orientals by trying to ape their habits. Let him treat the laws of others respectfully, but he will himself meet with a far greater respect if he adheres strictly to his own. For a woman this rule is of the first importance since a woman can never disguise herself effectually. That she should be known to come of a great and honoured stock, whose customs are inviolable, is her best claim to consideration.'

As her fluency in Arabic increased she would strike up conversations with the most unlikely, and sometimes the most unsavoury, people for the sheer joy of being able to speak to them in their own language. She refused ever to admit that the wild, foreign lands in which she chose to wander might hold lurking dangers for a solitary female traveller, and the only time she found it a disadvantage to be a woman was when she realised, to her fury, that she was not physically strong enough to administer a much-needed whipping to some particularly lazy servants. As she explained to Hugh, however, there were some feminine accoutrements that it suited her very well to abandon.

> The chief comfort of this journey is my masculine saddle, both to me and to my horse. Never, never again will I travel on anything else; I haven't known real ease in riding till now. Till I speak people always think I am a man. You mustn't think I haven't got a most elegant and decent divided skirt, however, but as all men wear skirts of sorts too, that doesn't serve to distinguish me.

Of the many qualities and characteristics for which Gertrude would be remembered, one of the most indelible would be her passion for clothes. Vita Sackville-West recalled first meeting Gertrude in Constantinople 'where she had arrived straight out of the desert, with all the evening dresses and cutlery that she insisted on taking with her on her wanderings'. Before she left London she already had a reputation for never being seen wearing the same dress twice to parties and throughout her years in the desert her letters home nearly always included an urgent request for some or other indispensable item for her wardrobe. 'I wish I had brought more clothes,' was a recurring cry and poor Florence must have come to dread reading the words, 'Could you possibly send me . . .' for they would inevitably mean her having to trail up to 'Marte of Conduit Street' for 'a stripey silk gown' or 'a winter hat – dark violet would be perfect'.

★   ★   ★   ★

By June 1900, having visited Palmyra to explore the ruins and Baalbek to see the cedars of Lebanon, Gertrude was ready to return home. 'But you know, dearest father, I shall be back here before long. One doesn't keep away from the East when one has got into it this far.' In fact it would be another five years before she returned to the Middle East for more than just a fleeting visit. She was not yet ready to commit herself to just one corner of the world, however fascinating that corner had proved to be. There were still too many things to see and do elsewhere.

For instance there were mountains to climb – literally. Her visits to the Alps with Hugh in 1893 and 1899 had whetted her appetite for the high peaks, and not long after her return from the stony wastes of Syria she was 'enjoying herself madly' in the snowy wastes of Switzerland, gaining a reputation for herself as a skilled and courageous climber.

And still she whirled on. In 1902 she took time off mountaineering to travel round the world for a second time with her half-brother Hugo. They attended the Great Durbar in Delhi in January 1903 as guests of the Viceroy, Lord Curzon. From India they travelled through Burma and Java to Hong Kong, China and Japan, Gertrude apparently swallowing each new language whole as if it were an aspirin. In America they paused just long enough for her to scale a few tempting peaks in the Rockies and by July they were back in England.

Here, at last, it began to seem that she had had enough of travelling just for the sake of it. Seeing the sights, learning the languages and being sumptuously entertained by ambassadors – even if most of them were relations or family friends – had its limitations. What Gertrude needed now was mental stimulation; something that would challenge her brain as the mountains and the deserts challenged her body.

A chance meeting in Paris provided her with exactly that. Salomon Reinach, philologist, archaeologist and art historian, was the 'profoundly knowledgeable' custodian of the National Museum at Saint Germain-en-Laye. He was a small, dapper and immensely charming man in his mid-forties who had only two passions outside his work; very beautiful women and very clever women. His relationships with them were rarely physical – he was happily married to a doctor who was both beautiful and clever; he just revelled in their company. He collected women friends as lovingly and as expertly as he collected Byzantine mosaics or ancient Egyptian manuscripts. He found Gertrude irresistible – and the feeling was mutual.

We talked without ceasing for four hours. He is a remarkable man who . . . knows everything. He gave me a letter of introduction to one of the directors of the Bibliothèque Nationale and when I went there today I was welcomed with open arms. I spent the whole day there studying manuscripts. What joy – I should like to do nothing else for six months.

Inspired by Reinach's apparently boundless knowledge, and with his wholehearted encouragement, Gertrude decided to do some research into the ruins that had so fascinated her in Syria. For three weeks she lived in libraries and museums, and her letters to Hugh reflect her delight in this new experience. 'Yesterday I went with Reinach to a Byzantine museum that is not yet open to the public'; 'I spent the afternoon in the Louvre'; 'I am going to dine with Reinach and spend the evening in his library'; 'What a dear man – I have learned more in these few days than I should have learned by myself in a year'; 'last night he set me a sort of examination – and I think I passed. Reinach was much pleased, but then he loves me so dearly that perhaps he is not a good judge.'

In fact Reinach was a superb judge – and by gently prodding Gertrude towards what he knew should be her vocation he was setting her on a course to which she would remain true for the rest of her life. Soon after she had 'passed his exam' he commissioned her to write a series of pieces for his scholarly journal, *Revue Archéologique*, and by January 1905 she was back in the Middle East.

> Haifa, January 25th. It is a pleasure to be speaking Arabic again. I feel it coming back in a flood and every time I open my lips expecting toads, pearls come out – at least seed pearls. I thought today as I was strolling round the bazaars buying various odds and ends for my journey what a pleasure it is to be in the East almost as part of it, to know it all as I know it now. To be able to tell from the accent and dress of the people where they come from and exchange the proper greeting as one passes. Oh I've had such a day. I've lunched with Persians, drunk tea with my horse dealer, spent hours in conversation with my landlord and visited everyone I know in Haifa. I'm off tomorrow morning.

Of all the journeys she would make through the Middle East, this one was without doubt the most pleasurable and carefree. Thanks to Reinach, archaeology had become her consuming passion, and thanks to his commission for articles she had a valid reason to indulge it. Her travel plans were somewhat vague; but this too added to the charm of the adventure.

From Jerusalem she intended to follow her earlier route to Damascus via the mountains of the Jebel Druse, and then head northwards through Syria and into present-day Turkey. Relying partly on her own knowledge and partly on information gleaned from people she met along the way, she would be free to make whatever detours and diversions would take her to the most interesting ruins. And she had all the time in the world.

★   ★   ★   ★

With three muleteers and a cook for company, she leapt onto her 'masculine saddle' and rode out of Jerusalem on 5 February with a whoop of joy. 'The west wind swept up from the Mediterranean, shouted the news of rain to the city and raced onwards, followed by all the hounds of the storm. No one with life in his body could stay in on such a day.' They crossed the Jordan river near Jericho over 'the wooden bridge that leads from Occident to Orient' and by the end of the first day Gertrude was 'deep in the gossip of the East − I could have wept for joy at listening to it again.'

She made friends with her customary panache, expecting − and finding − a welcome in every village and round every camp-fire from Amman to Aleppo. Predictably it was the men whose company she sought. In Arabia as in Europe, male acceptance of her presence, male approval of her endeavours and male acknowledgement of her ability and prowess in fields that had traditionally been their own, were the only valid criteria by which she was prepared to be judged. It would have been no triumph for her to be accepted by or to excel amongst other women, even at home; as far as she was concerned they comprised neither worthy competition nor stimulating company. She was shockingly dismissive of her sex *en masse* and in later years would be a vigorous campaigner against women's suffrage. It was as if she felt that those women who had a contribution to make would make it anyway, and those who had nothing to offer did not need to be given a voice. Since she had little time for her fellow women of the Christian Occident, it is not surprising that she barely seemed to notice the cloistered and far more repressed women of the predominantly Islamic Orient.

Although antiquities were her priority her letters home over the next four months reveal her as a compulsive gatherer of every kind of information. They overflowed with detailed observations on everything from religious bigotry to goat husbandry, from the patterns of the stars to the meanings of words to the colour of flowers. They talked of battles and blood-feuds, of history, geography and politics. But they made little or no mention of life in the Middle East as it was lived by women.

For the first week of her journey it rained. Beyond Amman the rain became so heavy that they were forced to take shelter, mules, horses, tents and all, in a large cave which was already occupied by a group of men from the Beni Sakhr tribe. Driven out of their black tents by the weather, but leaving their wives and children to shift for themselves amid the leaks and the drips and the mud, these Bedouin tribesmen were comfortably ensconced round a large crackling fire drinking coffee. Gertrude, an inveterate smoker herself, made her contribution to the 'conviviality of the party' by handing round cigarettes from her own supply, and before long 'a friendly feeling had been established between me and the men of the Beni Sakhr.'

Near Salt she stopped to watch men of the Shararat tribe buying corn from the Beni Sakhr. 'But for my incongruous presence and the lapse of a few thousand years they might have been the sons of Jacob come down into Egypt to bicker over the weight of the sacks with their brother Joseph.' In the town of Salt itself she presented herself at the house of 'the brother-in-law of the daughter of the man who used to teach me Arabic who promised he knew someone who could guide me into the Jebel Druse.'

She wanted to penetrate into the heart of the Jebel Druse mountains for the same reason that Alexandra David-Neel wanted to go to Lhasa – because it was forbidden. The unorthodox and fiercely independent Druses had never accepted Turkish domination and, partly for geographical reasons, the Turks were prepared to leave them largely to their own devices. But foreign travellers were discouraged from entering their domain for fear they would spread sedition and dissent. Gertrude could not resist the challenge.

> It's awfully amusing – we feel quite like conspirators and my servants fully enter into the fun of the thing. If I can just put myself in communication with the Druses all will be well. Once into their country I'll move quickly and it will be difficult for the Turks to catch me, for they are horribly afraid of the Druses.

Setting out before dawn and giving a wide berth to villages, she was guided by the 'friend of the brother-in-law of the daughter of her old Arabic teacher' across the desert and up into the forbidden hills. From now on she was assured of a warm welcome – anyone who could outwit the Turk was automatically a true friend of the Druse. Word of her approach travelled ahead of her and she wandered happily through the Jebel Druse for three weeks. 'Some interest surrounds me for I am the first foreign woman who has ever been in these parts.' The fact that the stony plain round Saleh, in the heart of the Jebel Druse, was strewn with the ruins of villages deserted since the Mohammedan invasion of the seventh century was a welcome bonus. The sight of this archaeological happy hunting ground diverted Gertrude's thoughts from her triumph over authority and soon had her bustling about with notebook, pencil and tape measure. 'Without doubt this is a wonderful world. I began my day by copying inscriptions – I found several Greek, one Cufic and one Nabathean – Lord knows what it means but I put it faithfully down and the learned shall read it.'

It was cold in the mountains and she was extremely thankful that she had brought with her not only a fur coat but a hot water bottle. Her luggage, now as ever, also included enough china and cutlery to allow her to dine in style even in the back of beyond, and a collapsible bath. At the end of every day her servants lit a fire, the canvas tub was erected in her tent and Gertrude was soon wallowing in 'the greatest luxury of the camp'.

Near the town of Salkhad she was invited to partake of more than the usual hospitality. She had just finished dinner and was debating whether it was too cold to write up her diary when 'a sound of savage singing broke upon the night. It was a call to arms.' Pausing only to grab her fur coat, Gertrude rushed out into the moonlight to find a crowd of Druse men and boys staging a ferocious demonstration against the Turks.

> They were all armed with swords and knives and were shouting as though the fury of their anger would never end. One of them saw me standing watching and strode up to me and, raising his sword above his head, shouted 'Lady, the English and the Druse are one'. I said 'Praise be to God we too are a fighting race.' Indeed at that moment there seemed to be no finer thing than to go out and kill your enemy. When the swearing in of warriors, of whom I now seemed to be one, was over we ran down the hill together to the edge of the town.

For a while Gertrude allowed herself to be swept along by the wild-eyed crowd. But she knew there was a Turkish official based in the town and when it looked as though the demonstrators were heading for his residence, commonsense prevailed. 'I turned away into the shadows and ran back to my tents and became a European again, bent on peaceful pursuits and unacquainted with the naked primitive passions of mankind.' Outwitting the Turkish authorities was one thing, taking part in demonstrations against them was quite another. Should word of her presence at such a gathering ever reach their ears, they might find it hard to believe in the innocence of her journey.

As the time approached for her to move on, Gertrude began to wonder whether her detour into the Jebel Druse had, after all, been very wise. Such capricious antics were not really appropriate to her new role as a serious student of archaeology; it would be a tragedy if they were to place the rest of her planned journey in jeopardy. So when she reached Damascus a week after leaving Salkhad, she went straight to the Turkish Governor of the city, confessed her sin and apologised profusely for her lack of respect for his authority. The Governor was courtesy personified. He assured her that her apologies were unnecessary and that the whole of Syria was at her disposal – she was free to travel wherever she wished. But she was soon to discover that this was just a manner of speaking. For the duration of her stay in Damascus every time she went out she was followed by a policeman who was commissioned to watch over her safety, and when she left the city to continue her travels the Governor announced that he was sending an armed escort to guard so distinguished a traveller.

To admit that she had made a mess of things was more than Gertrude could manage – so she chose to take this surveillance as a compliment to her standing rather than as a subtle punishment for her escapade in the Jebel Druse.

> I hereby renounce in despair the hope of ever again being a simple, happy traveller. The Turkish government has decided that I am a great swell and nothing will persuade them to the contrary. It is boring to tears and very expensive, but what am I to do?

Fortunately official interest in her activities waned once she was beyond the jurisdiction of the Governor of Damascus and she was able to revert to being a 'simple, happy traveller'.

*   *   *   *

Copying inscriptions, measuring pillars and writing up notes, Gertrude worked her way northwards. As her interest in archaeology grew so her reactions to her surroundings changed. Leaving the Jebel Druse she had remarked that the peasants were to be congratulated for 'pushing forward the limits of cultivation . . . and proving conclusively the value of land'. Touring the sites of northern Syria only a few weeks later she began to see such progress as a threat. The sight of families making their homes amid ancient ruins and planting the previously uncultivated land around with corn would 'no doubt warm the heart of the lover of humanity, but it sends a cold chill through the breast of the archaeologist. There is no obliterator like the plough-share and no destroyer like the peasant who seeks cut stones to build his hovel.'

Pausing at Aleppo only for long enough to pay off her Arabic-speaking Lebanese muleteers and engage some Turkish-speaking replacements, she left Syria and entered Asia Minor. Her own Turkish vocabulary at that time consisted of three words – egg, milk and piastre – 'but I have to talk Turkish, there's nothing else for it. I make a preposterous mess of it but I hope in a week or two I shall begin to scrub along.' Needless to say by the time she reached Konia a month later she was chatting away quite happily to all and sundry in her latest tongue.

Her introduction to Turkey and its people gave her a very favourable first impression. 'I have fallen a hopeless victim to the Turk; he is the most charming of mortals.' But the new team of servants she had engaged in Aleppo forced her into an early qualification.

> Though [Turks] are the most delightful of acquaintances they are the worst of servants. They will take any amount of trouble for you for nothing, but once you hire them to work, not a hand's turn will they do. At the hands of the Turkish muleteers I suffer tortures. They get into camp and when they have unloaded the mules they sit down on one of the packs and light a cigarette with an air of

impartial and wholly unconcerned benevolence. I have gone to the lengths of dislodging them with the lash of my crop, freely applied. It makes no difference; they stroll on to the next pack and take up a position there, smiling cheerfully all the while. There are moments when being a woman increases one's difficulties. What they need is a good beating – and that's what they would get if I were a man.

Among this unco-operative crew, however, was one gem. 'Fattuh, bless him, is the best servant I have ever had, ready to cook my dinner, push a mule or dig out an inscription with equal alacrity and to tell me endless tales of travel as we ride, for he began life as a muleteer at the age of ten and knows every inch of ground from Aleppo to Baghdad.' Fattuh would be Gertrude's companion and servant on every journey she made for the next eleven years.

Rounding off this journey with a two-week exploration of the ruined Byzantine churches of Anatolia, Gertrude arrived in Konia in the middle of May to a fortuitous meeting. 'I found there Professor Ramsay, who knows more about this country than any other man, and we fell into each other's arms and made great friends.' She was already familiar with Professor [later Sir William] Ramsay's work and knew he was thinking of undertaking an extensive archaeological and historical investigation of the Anatolian churches. Before she left for England she persuaded Ramsay to let her join his expedition planned for the following year.

In 1906 she published *The Desert and The Sown*, the account of her journey through Syria and Asia Minor. With the popular success of this book, and the academic accolades that greeted her second, *The Thousand and One Churches*, co-written with Ramsay in 1908, her reputation as a writer and archaeologist was established.

★   ★   ★   ★

'The incomparable Fattuh', her Armenian Christian 'gem' from Aleppo, had run her camp while she worked on the Anatolian churches with Ramsay in 1907. He was with her too in 1909 when she spent a further six months studying the Roman and Byzantine ruins of Mesopotamia, and he was in charge of her little caravan when she made a breakneck crossing of the Syrian desert from Damascus to Baghdad in 1911. But in December 1913, as she set out from Damascus on the most ambitious journey of her career, Fattuh was not by her side. He was at home in Aleppo suffering from typhoid. In the normal way Gertrude would have delayed her departure until he had recovered from his illness. But this time she could not wait.

Her destination was Ha'il, the desert city 500 miles south of Damascus in the heart of what is now Saudi Arabia. It was a journey she had been planning for some years, but it involved travelling through country that was geographically harsh and politically unstable. She had been forced to pick her moment carefully.

> Dearest beloved father, my plans are developing and luck seems to be on my side. An almost incredible tranquillity reigns in the desert – the oldest enemies are at peace and there have been excellent autumn rains so that I shall find both grass and surface water. Bassan found me some riding camels going cheap in Damascus – an incredible stroke of good luck as I thought I should have to transport myself somewhere into the wilds and haggle for camels there. I now have twenty camels of my very own and feel rather like an Arab sheikh myself.

As far as Hugh and Florence were concerned she was merely fulfilling an ambition she had cherished for more than eight years, and she was careful to maintain the illusion. But her serenity was a sham; her cheerfulness a charade. Gertrude was miserably and hopelessly in love.

Major Charles Hotham Montagu Doughty-Wylie of the Royal Welch Fusiliers, known to his friends as Richard or Dick, was the nephew of that most famous of Arabian travellers, Charles Doughty. Gertrude had first met him in 1909 when he was British Consul in Konia in western Turkey, and their paths had crossed again three years later in London when he was appointed Director-in-Chief of the Red Cross relief organisation to victims of the Balkan war. Their private meetings were few and fleeting, but by the end of 1912 they were corresponding with increasing ardour. His letters to Gertrude reveal the depth of their mutual attraction.

> My dear Gertrude, this morning arrived your book and a letter. The book I have read all day – it's perfectly wonderful and I love it and you. I can't write about it yet – and it would take the book of my soul, never written, to answer it. . . . Would you like me to write you a love letter? To say in some feeble whisper what the mind outside is shouting – to say how glad and gratified and humble I am when I think of you? . . . I kiss your hands and your feet, dear woman of my heart, you are delightful and wise and strong, and such as my soul loveth.

On the face of it the two were perfectly suited; the distinguished soldier and diplomat and the brilliant scholar, writer and traveller. But there was no future in their love – for Richard was already married. To have left his wife would have been to sacrifice both his private reputation and his professional career, and however deeply he might be in love with Gertrude, he was not prepared to expose them all to the inevitable scandal. For two years Gertrude had prayed for the impossible. Suddenly, she could bear it no longer.

Since the death of Henry Cadogan in 1893 she had turned her back on all thoughts of marriage and concentrated on her travels. Now, at the age of forty-five, the comfortable assumption that she was in complete command of her own destiny had been shattered. All her old dreams had returned to haunt – and to taunt – her; the redoubtable lady was running away. 'I want to cut all links with the world, and this is the best and wisest way to do it.'

Her father Hugh, once such a vigorous traveller himself, had for some time been confined to the house by ill-health and could now only travel vicariously through the wanderings of his famous daughter. She was determined not to allow her private heartbreak to interfere with his enjoyment; therefore she continued to write to him, as before, merely of the joys and vicissitudes of the desert. Only Sir Valentine Chirol, foreign editor of *The Times* and a lifelong friend of Gertrude's, knew the real extent of her misery – and he was the only person in whom she was prepared to confide.

> If you knew the way I had paced backwards and forwards along the floor of hell for the last few months, you would think me right to try any way out. I don't know that it is an ultimate way out but it is worth trying. As I have told you before it is mostly my fault, but that does not prevent it from being an irretrievable misfortune – for both of us. But I am turning away from it now, and time deadens even the keenest things. The road and the dawn, the sun, the wind and the rain, the camp fire under the stars, sleep, and the road again – we'll see what these can do. If they don't cure, then I know of nothing that can.

Having made her decision she had to leave at once, before anything or anyone could change her mind. Thus, in Damascus, she had to set off without Fattuh.

She had never intended this, or indeed any of her other journeys, to be a pioneering venture. Several European travellers had visited Ha'il before, of whom William Gifford Palgrave, Wilfred and Lady Anne Blunt, and Charles Doughty are the best known. But Gertrude never travelled as an explorer – she travelled rather as a scholar and archaeologist, to observe and interpret first as a student and then as an expert all aspects of Middle Eastern culture. Her journey to Ha'il was another step in this learning process, albeit a fairly adventurous one, and she never made any further claims for it than that.

The first stage, south from Damascus round the mountains of the Jebel Druse to Madeba at the north-east corner of the Dead Sea, was familiar territory. This part of the route was still too close to civilisation to satisfy her longing for complete isolation, and her frustration was compounded by the absence of Fattuh. 'When you have no man with you who has ever travelled with a European you can guess what it is like. I had to show them [her new servants] everything and find everything myself. . . . They did not know how my English tents went up nor even how to boil an egg.' By the time they reached Ziza three weeks later she had managed 'by dint of patience and timely instruction' to break them in almost to her satisfaction.

Had it been possible she would have given even this small outpost of civilisation a wide berth – her resolve was still vulnerable and might disintegrate at a word or a touch. But the Damascus–Hijaz railway passed through Ziza and it had been arranged that Fattuh would join her there. Gritting her teeth she forced herself to ask at the station for any letters. There were none. And for the next two months at least she would be beyond the reach of even the most determined postal service. Half glad and half sorry that there was no desperate, irresistible plea from Richard for her to return, she set about provisioning her caravan for the long road ahead. Once Fattuh had appeared 'still looking pale and thin but with a clean bill of health from his doctor – I have missed him dreadfully and he is in the seventh heaven at being back with us', she was ready to go.

> And so we set out. My hosts clasped me by the hand and sent us forth with many deep-voiced blessings and I turned my face to Arabia.

★   ★   ★   ★

In order to reach Ha'il, which lay in the Nejd, or highlands of Central Arabia, Gertrude first had to cross the broad bands of assorted desert that bounded the Great Sandy Desert far to the south. According to William Gifford Palgrave, who made the journey to Ha'il in 1862, these desert-rings were easily distinguishable one from another, and even the first, and easiest, offered a less than inviting prospect to the traveller.

> South of the Syrian waste, and reaching from the Dead Sea in the West to the valley of the Euphrates in the East, runs a broad belt of level country, hard and stony, with few sources of water, even in the winter season. . . . Before us and on either hand extended one weary plain in a black monotony of lifelessness. Only on all sides lakes of mirage lay mocking the eye with their clear and deceptive outline, whilst here and there some dark basaltic rock, cropping up at random, was magnified by the refraction of the heated atmosphere into the semblance of a fantastic crag or over-hanging mountain. Dreary land of death, in which even the face of an enemy were almost a relief amid such utter solitude. (W.G. Palgrave, *Personal Narrative of a Year's Journey through Central and Eastern Arabia*, 1868.)

In theory this emptiness was exactly what Gertrude wanted. The harder the route and the more arduous each day's journey, the further away she would feel from the source of her misery and the less time she would have to think. In a brave effort to sustain the customary jaunty tone of her letters, she wrote to Hugh and Florence, 'It is a fine country . . . and I am enjoying myself mightily.' But to Valentine Chirol she wrote very differently.

> I have known loneliness in solitude now, for the first time, and in the long days of camel riding and the long evenings of winter camping, my thoughts have gone wandering far from the camp fire into places which I wish were not so full of acute sensation. Sometimes I have gone to bed with a heart so heavy that I thought I could not carry it through the next day. Then comes the dawn, soft and beneficent, stealing over the wide plain and down the long slopes of the little hollows, and in the end it steals into my dark heart also. That's the best I can make of it, taught at least some wisdom by solitude, taught submission, and how to bear pain without crying out.

Two weeks of this 'dreary land of death' brought Gertrude and her caravan to the edge of the Wadi Sirhan. Literally translated as the Valley of the Wolves, the Wadi Sirhan is a long, sinuous depression stretching for nearly 100 miles south-eastwards into the next broad belt of more sandy desert. Although the valley could by no stretch of the imagination be called fertile, its less than absolute barrenness and the relatively easy access to underground water meant that it formed the main trade route from the north to the first great oasis settlement of the south – Jof. But as Gertrude well knew, it was the lawless, turbulent politics of this region that had made the route to Ha'il so notorious.

The three main tribes of the Wadi Sirhan region were the Sukhur, the Ruwalla and the Howeitat. Of these, the Howeitat were currently the most powerful and their feud of the moment was with the Ruwalla. For the duration of this feud the third tribe, the Sukhur, held an uneasy middle ground, certain of nothing save that their respite from the hostile attentions of the other two would be short-lived. Any passing traveller, no matter how neutral his stance or conciliatory his conduct, was liable to find himself turned on by any one of these tribes, by all three, or indeed by half a dozen lesser ones.

Gertrude was unalarmed. She knew the Arabs. She understood their complicated inter-tribal relationships; she was familiar with the customs and courtesies of the desert; and above all she knew their language. She had never yet, in all her years of travel, met the situation with which she could not cope. But there was another reason for her unconcern. 'Occasionally my eyes strain themselves to catch a glimpse of the future, and sometimes I do indeed wonder whether I shall come out of this adventure alive. But the doubt has no shadow of anxiety in it – I am profoundly indifferent.'

Almost inevitably, as they were wending their way through the Wadi Sirhan they were attacked by a raiding party of Sukhur tribesmen. Shrieking horsemen with matted black hair swept out of the sand dunes and whirled about their caravan, shooting their rifles into the air 'like men insane'. Her servants were forced to dismount and the raiders stripped them of their guns, cartridge belts and cloaks. Once upon a time Gertrude would have marched out in front of them, whip in hand, and told them exactly what she thought of their manners. Not any more. 'As there was nothing to be done but sit quiet and watch events, that was what I did.'

When one of Gertrude's camelherds recognised one of the members of the raiding party, the whole stramash evaporated. The shrieking horsemen were transformed into courteous gentlemen of the desert, the stolen guns were returned and the two groups 'rode on together in quiet and serenity'. However when a scout reported a large camp of the Howeitat over the next hill, the Sukhur themselves evaporated. Since her companions were still in a state of shock after the last encounter, it was left to Gertrude to introduce herself and her party to the Sheikh of the Howeitat and assure him that they were merely harmless travellers. So successful were her efforts that by the evening the Sheikh was swearing his eternal friendship.

The Abu Tayyi are the great sheikhs of the Howeitat and Muhammad Abu Tayyi is a magnificent person, tall and big with a flashing look – not like the slender Bedouin sitting round the fire. He carries the Howeitat reputation for dare-devilry written on his face – I should not like to meet him in anger. But he is a good fellow and I trust him. We spent three days in his company. Of an evening we sat in his big tent – he is an important person – and I listened to the tales and songs of the desert and the romantic adventures of the princes of Nejd. Muhammad sat beside me on the rugs which were spread on the clean soft sand, his great figure wrapped in a sheepskin coat. Long after dark the 'nagas', the camel-mothers, came home with their calves and crouched down in the sand outside the open tent. Muhammad got up, drew his robes about him and went out into the night with a huge wooden bowl, which he brought back to me full to the brim of camel's milk, a most delectable drink. I fancy that when you have drunk the milk of the naga over the campfire of the Abu Tayyi you are baptised of the desert and there is no other salvation for you. They were interesting days and prolonged beyond my intention for this reason.

By now it was early February – nearly two months since Gertrude had left Damascus – and she was beginning to find a serenity of sorts in the desert. The dilemmas she had to confront and the decisions she had to reach were all of the moment. Which was the best way to go? How far was it likely to be to the next water? Why was this camel so troublesome and that one ailing? It was a blessed relief to be faced with such familiar and absorbing problems and to know that the answer to each one could be found merely by referring back to past experience. If only all her troubles could have been so clear-cut and soluble.

Muhammad Abu Tayyi warned her against travelling to Jof. The route, he assured her, was 'infested by raiders from the Ruwalla who would fall upon us by night and undoubtedly rob us, if not worse'. At this alarming prospect her companions begged her to accept Muhammad's offer of a guide to take them south on a direct route through the rolling sand dunes of the Nefud to the mountains of Nejd. She had no means of knowing whether the stories of the Ruwalla were true but 'I take it to be against the rules of the game to persist in taking a road against which I am warned by all.' So she agreed to change her plans.

She was not sorry to miss Jof, a town of which she had heard no great reports. Muhammad's alternative route was untried and empty and held dangers of its own, foremost amongst which was the probable lack of fodder or water for the camels. Yet it had an attraction for Gertrude in that it was also unmapped. Since her earliest days as a student of archaeology she had had a passion for drawing plans and making maps. Theodolite and compass were standard items in her luggage and, as she explained to her father, the direct route to Nejd gave her an ideal opportunity to use them.

The Nefud is a great stretch of sandhills 7 or 8 days journey across. I am glad to see this famous wilderness, but the going is very heavy – up and down endless ridges of soft pale sand. The business of mapmaking, far from being a trouble, is a great amusement and alleviation in the long hours of riding and walking, though there are few points for my compass bearings. I should think that as the crow flies we barely cover a mile in an hour, but I don't mind. I never tire of looking at the red gold landscape and wondering at its amazing desolation and I sometimes wonder whether there is anywhere that I am at all anxious to reach. I feel as if I had been born and bred in the Nefud and had known no other world. Is there any other?

But the novelty did not last long. The slow pace of their progress, the monotony of the landscape, the stillness of the air, the pervading silence and above all her own profound unhappiness were a crushing combination. As they approached the southern limit of the Nefud she wrote in her diary, 'I am suffering from a severe fit of depression. . . . It's nothing [this journey] so far as any real addition to knowledge goes. . . . That which has chanced to lie upon my path for the last ten days is not worth mentioning – two wells, and really I can think of nothing else. I fear, when I come to the end of it I shall say "It was a waste of time". This reflection is discouraging and, like most of our wisest reflections, it comes too late.'

Her depression lasted for the rest of her journey. By the time she reached Ha'il at the end of February she was bone-weary. Her great journey into the heart of Arabia had failed on all counts – there had been nothing remarkable to achieve either archaeologically or cartographically, and her heartsick longing for Richard had been intensified rather than eased by the time and distance that separated them.

Even Ha'il itself was a disappointment. Instead of being greeted by the Amir, with whom she had hoped to establish her usual cordial relationship, she was met by his uncle, Ibrahim al Rashid, with the news that the Amir was away on a raiding party and might be gone for a month. Ibrahim treated her with courtesy and showed her to a guest house on the edge of the town. But the following morning when she set out to make a tour of Ha'il she was stopped by the gatekeepers who told her that she was not allowed to leave the house without permission. 'I am a prisoner, you understand.'

The reason for this unpleasant turn of events was that the Rashids were in a state of nervous tension bordering on panic. Ever since their rivals, the Sauds, had recaptured the town of Riyadh and ousted the Rashids ten years earlier, the power of the Rashids had been on the wane. The intervening years had seen an ever more bitter struggle for power between the various branches of the family – successive Amirs had been murdered and some-times their whole households with them. Even now the current Amir was travelling northwards with the express intention of murdering his uncle. If those who were left behind were suspicious of even their nearest relatives, how much more suspicious would they naturally be of a stranger who appeared from nowhere and for no apparent reason.

> So I sat in honourable captivity and the days were weary long. The tales round the fire were all of murder, and the air whispered of murder. In Ha'il murder is like the spilling of milk and not one of the sheikhs but feels his head sitting unsteadily on his shoulders. It gets on your nerves when you sit day after day between high mud walls and I thank heaven that my nerves are not very responsive. They kept me awake only one night out of the ten but I will not conceal from you that there were hours of considerable anxiety.

Using the niceties of Arab etiquette to her own advantage, Gertrude won a few hours' respite from her weary imprisonment by insisting on repaying Ibrahim's visit, knowing he could not refuse to see her. She presented him with bolts of silk which she had brought with her as gifts and gave him also her second best pair of binoculars and a revolver for the absent Amir. Casually she dropped every influential Arab name she could recall into their conversation. She murmured about the probable reactions of her powerful friends to the news of her imprisonment, and finally she managed to persuade Ibrahim, if not to let her leave, at least to allow her a small measure of freedom within Ha'il.

> Next day came word from the Amir's mother inviting me to visit her. I went, riding solemnly through the silent moonlit streets of this strange place, and

passed two hours, taken straight from the Arabian Nights, with the women of the palace. I imagine there are few places left where you can see the unadulterated East as it has lived for centuries, and of these few Ha'il is one. There they were, those women, wrapped in Indian brocades, hung with jewels, served by slaves, and there was not one single thing about them which betrayed the existence of Europe or Europeans – except me. I was the blot.

Ten days of waiting stretched her patience beyond its limits. Gertrude lost her temper. She bribed her gatekeepers to let her pass and marched to Ibrahim's house where, abandoning Arab convention and flowery Oriental speeches, she spoke her mind and left abruptly, convinced that she had just signed her own death warrant. To her utter astonishment, within an hour of returning to her room one of Ibrahim's servants appeared with the news that she had permission to leave Ha'il straightaway.

I replied with great dignity that I was much obliged and that I did not intend to leave till the next day for I wished to see the palace and the town by daylight. The following day I sent for my camels and spent some hours being shown everything I wanted to see. Why they gave way then, or why they had not given way before, I cannot guess. But who can look into their dark minds? So now I go to Baghdad. After careful enquiries I feel sure that the road south is not possible this year – the tribes are up and the road is barred. So Ha'il must suffice.

Despite the obstacles, the road south would have presented the Gertrude of ten years before an irresistible challenge. But not now. Her heart was no longer in her journey; to prolong it would be pointless, so she turned away.

From Ha'il it took her twenty-five days to reach Baghdad and she arrived at the home of the British Vice-Consul on 29 March 1914. She was so exhausted, both mentally and physically, that she could find little pleasure even in hearing English spoken for the first time in more than three months. To make matters worse – or better, she could not decide which – there was a whole pile of letters waiting for her from Richard who was now British Consul in Addis Ababa. Reading them it was instantly obvious that separation had changed his feelings as little as it had changed hers. The future promised to be as unhappy as the past; and her journey to Ha'il had, indeed, solved nothing.

★   ★   ★   ★

Within six months of her return to England, Europe was at war. In the face of this new horror Gertrude threw her pride to the winds. Almost on her knees she wrote to Richard begging him, while they still had the chance, to leave his wife and go to her. But she knew he would not. They continued to correspond, but their meeting in London in February 1915 would be their last. Doughty-Wylie, by now a Lieutenant-Colonel, was killed by a sniper's bullet as he led his troops in a heroic assault on the beach at Gallipoli in April 1915. He was awarded a posthumous VC.

Gertrude's grief was too deep and too private to share with anyone. Not until three years had passed would she admit to her father that 'the sorrow at the back of everything deadens me to all else'. Maybe this was the secret behind the brittleness of her humour, the sharp edge to her tongue and the increasingly domineering manner that would give her, in years to come, such a formidable reputation.

With the outbreak of war Gertrude found her opinion and advice in constant demand and in November 1915 she was recruited into the Arab Bureau, the intelligence organisation established in Cairo to formulate British strategy in the Middle East. It was work for which she was ideally suited. She was already acquainted with most of the other members of the Bureau, including the soon-to-be-immortal T.E. Lawrence, whom she had first met on an archaeological dig in Syria in 1911. She was fluent in Arabic and had first-hand knowledge of the people and places under discussion. Her social and family connections gave her a direct line to many of the most influential figures in British politics. She was opinionated, highly articulate and – since Richard's death – not only free, but anxious to spend as little time as possible in England.

For the duration of the war she worked for the Arab Bureau in Cairo, Basra and Baghdad, and it was in Baghdad that she made her home for the rest of her life. In 1917 she was awarded the CBE for her contribution to Arab affairs and in 1918 came word that she had been awarded the Founder's Medal of the Royal Geographical Society – an honour that provoked her to comment, 'It was an absurd thing to give me; they must have been hard up for travellers this year.'

For four years after the war, in her role as Oriental Secretary to the British High Commissioner, Gertrude worked tirelessly towards the restructuring of the Middle East. The coronation of King Faisal of Iraq in 1921 was perhaps the greatest triumph of her career, and she attended the ceremonies as his personal and honoured guest. An American journalist who met her in Baghdad at this time described her as having 'nothing of the weather-beaten hardened explorer in her looks or bearing; she was all "Paris frocks and Mayfair manners".' In 1923, when she had no longer any part to play in the politics of the now autonomous country, she was content to revert to the passion of her youth, archaeology, and spent three years as Iraq's Director of Antiquities.

A questionmark will always remain over the manner of Gertrude's death. Even among her surviving relatives there is no consensus – some are inclined to believe that it was accidental, while others say they have always been sure it was suicide. Her health had become increasingly fragile during her long years in Iraq, and on her last visit to England in the summer of 1925 her doctors advised her not to return to Baghdad; but by now she felt more at home in Iraq than in England and she ignored their advice. Yet her physical frailty, and the knowledge that nothing could ever match the stimulation and excitement of the last ten years, were deeply depressing. 'Except for the museum I am not enjoying life at all,' she wrote in June 1926, 'it is a very lonely business living here now.'

She died on the morning of 12 July and was buried in the evening of the same day in the British cemetery in Baghdad.

★   ★   ★   ★

Gertrude had long ago dismissed her journey to Ha'il as a failure and her achievements as 'dust and ashes in one's hand – dead bones that look as if they would never rise and dance.' But amongst the sheaf of laudatory obituaries that appeared after her death was one that would put these into perspective. Its author was David Hogarth, chief of the Arab Bureau when Gertrude joined and President of the Royal Geographical Society at the time of her death.

> Her journey was a pioneer venture which not only put on the map a line of wells, before unplaced or unknown, but also cast much new light on the history of the Syrian desert frontiers. But perhaps the most valuable result consists in the mass of information that she accumulated about the tribal elements ranging between the Hejaz Railway on the one flank and the Sirhan and Nefud on the other, of which Lawrence, relying on her reports, made signal use in the Arab campaigns of 1917 and 1918. Her stay in Ha'il was fruitful of political information especially concerning both the recent history and the actual state of the Rashid house, and also its relations with the rival power of the Ibn Saud. Her information proved of great value during the war, when Ha'il had ranged itself with the enemy and was menacing our Euphratean flank. Miss Bell became, from 1915 onwards, the interpreter of all reports received from Central Arabia.

Of all the descriptions that remain of Gertrude Bell at various stages of her life, however, perhaps the words that would have pleased her most were those of a Bedouin sheikh with whom she negotiated a treaty in 1920.

> My brothers, you have heard what this woman has to say to us. She is only a woman, but y'Allah, she is a mighty and a valiant one. Now, we know that God has made all women inferior to men. If the women of the Angleez are like her, the men must be lions in strength and valour. We had better make peace with them.

CHAPTER SIX

'SCARCELY A SACRIFICE'
· *Daisy Bates* ·

he Nullarbor Plain covers 100 000 square miles of southern
Australia. It is an empty, scorching, barren expanse of scrub and
sand lying between the Great Victoria Desert to the north and the
vast seas of the Great Australian Bight to the south. At its western edge lies
the town of Kalgoorlie, scene of the famous goldrush, where in 1894 one
man jumped off his horse into a heap of nuggets and scooped up three-
quarters of a million pounds worth in two hours. It was in order to bring
this bonanza within reach of the eager prospectors of South Australia,
Victoria and New South Wales that, in the early years of this century, the
Trans-Australia Railway was built. The first train left Port Augusta for
Kalgoorlie, over 1000 miles away, in October 1917.

In the years that followed, many a west-bound passenger, roused from
his torpor by the maddening cloud of flies that invaded the carriage
whenever the train slowed to a halt, must have blinked twice at the sight
that met his eyes at Ooldea. Ooldea could hardly be called a station – it did
not even merit the term settlement. Four hundred miles out into the
middle of nowhere, Ooldea was just a stop, a siding where east and
west-bound trains could pass on the otherwise single track.

And yet there, beside the track, stood a small, dapper, elderly lady.
Immaculately dressed in a straw boater with full veil, long-sleeved white
blouse with a stiff collar and ribbon tie, ankle-length skirt and high-heeled
buttoned boots, she waited calmly in the full glare of the mid-day sun while
the guard sorted out her mail. Then she turned and walked away across the
sand-hills. Dismissing this improbable sight as a phantom of the heat-
shimmer, hats were tipped down over noses, limbs re-arranged on the seats,
and the passengers drifted back to sleep as the train drew out. But the lady
was no mirage. She was Mrs Daisy Bates, Justice of the Peace and Honorary
Protector of the Aborigines of Western and South Australia.

If there was any justice, the name of Daisy Bates would rank not far below those of Florence Nightingale and Mother Theresa in the international hall of fame. That it does not is a sad reflection of the continuing lack of international interest in the cause to which she devoted her life – the welfare of Australian aboriginals. But Daisy would not be surprised by this. She sought no fame for herself and expected no dramatic improvement in the fortunes of her protégés – indeed, she seriously believed that within a few years of her own death the full-blooded and truly tribal aborigine would no longer exist. For thirty-five years she worked not for the aborigine's right to an integrated role in Australian society, but to 'ease his passing'. She set herself up not as a bridge between palaeolithic man and the twentieth century, but as a barrier to protect the primitive from the civilised.

She failed, as she knew she would. The superficial attractions of the white man's world were too strong. Sadly, and with something of the fatalism inherent in the nature of the aborigines themselves, she watched the remnants of native tribes from all over Australia succumb to the ravages of the white man's diseases, to the easy solace of white man's drink and to the temptations of white man's crime. She fed and clothed the derelict and the starving, she nursed the syphilitic and the tubercular with profound compassion, and she held the hands of the dying and talked to them of the 'dreamtime', the aboriginal parable of creation. But she knew that there was nothing she or anyone else could do to save them.

She was not a missionary. She had no medical or sociological training, and she received little official support and no government funding for her work. She was not even Australian. Daisy Bates was an Irish journalist.

*   *   *   *

Daisy May O'Dwyer was born in 1859 in County Tipperary into the Protestant Irish landed gentry. Her mother died while she was still a baby and Daisy and her sister and brother were brought up ostensibly by their slightly eccentric grandmother but in fact by a succession of rosy-cheeked, uneducated and highly superstitious Irish maids. On the death of her grandmother, when Daisy was in her early teens, she was sent to live in Scotland with Sir Francis and Lady Outram, old friends of the O'Dwyer family, who welcomed her as if she was another daughter. In the company of the four Outram girls, and under the guidance of a formidable governess, the red-haired, freckle-faced Daisy made the transition from cheerful hoyden to stylish young lady. Together they studied deportment and elocution and learned French and German; they whirled round the cultural shrines of Europe and the social shrines of London, Edinburgh and Dublin; they danced at débutante parties and were presented at court to the Prince and Princess of Wales.

Despite this seemingly boundless energy, Daisy's health was not robust. Every winter brought on recurring colds and respiratory problems; her doctor detected signs of consumption and suggested she would benefit from a drier, sunnier climate. Her father had died in 1880 leaving her a comfortable inheritance and she had a long-standing invitation to visit friends in Queensland. So in 1884, aged twenty-five, she left for Australia.

Australia suited her to perfection. Here, in the land of pioneers and settlers, 'polite' did not automatically mean 'stuffy', the sophisticated did not look down on the homely and the formal lived happily alongside the easy-going. Elegant little Daisy O'Dwyer, with her beautiful clothes, graceful manners and sparkling smile, was welcomed into urban drawing room as warmly as into outback homestead. But it was the outback that she really loved. Consumption forgotten, she found herself learning to muster cattle on horseback, to kill snakes, keep a look-out for crocodiles in the creeks and to cook on an open bush fire. Carried away by the adventure, she made what she would later refer to as the one great mistake of her life.

In December 1884, six months after her arrival in Australia, she attended a rodeo in New South Wales. One man dominated every competition: horse races, bare-back riding, wood chopping, bronco busting, sheep handling – Jack Bates won them all. The eyes of every girl in the crowd were drawn to the tall, handsome stockman who walked away with prize after prize. Daisy was no exception. She announced to her laughing friends that she was going to marry him; and two months later she did.

Jack Bates seemed to personify everything that Daisy found exciting about Australia. He was young, strong and practical. With her money and his knowledge of the country they could join the brave pioneers of the outback whose enterprising spirit she so much admired; they would buy one of the vast tracts of empty land being offered to settlers by the government, build a homestead of their own and turn it into a profitable cattle station. So taken was she by this vision of domestic bliss that it was easy to find glamour in Jack's unkempt appearance and to interpret his taciturnity as an indication of a deep and interesting character. It was even possible not to complain when he celebrated their precipitate marriage by setting off on a six-month cattle drove without her.

But if the dream could survive his departure and his absence, it could not survive his return. Sober reflection revealed Jack as a man of little imagination and less ambition, content just to drift from one droving job to another and with no intention of settling down; a man to whom a wife was just a female creature who stayed at home while he wandered and who catered for his various physical needs when he chose to reappear; a man's man in what was, and would remain, a man's country. The romance evaporated, Jack headed off into the sunset on the heels of another herd of cattle and Daisy was left alone in their small surburban house in Sydney to contemplate the enormity of her 'error of judgement'.

The birth of their son in 1886 brought her no comfort. Daisy had few maternal instincts; young Arnold looked like Jack from the start and showed signs of being as dull and unimaginative as his father. For nine years she stayed in Australia trying desperately to salvage some sort of contentment from the mess. She used her inheritance to buy a property in Western Australia and even got as far as stocking it with cattle in an effort to make Jack settle down – but Jack had forgotten their dream; he was a drover not a settler and returned, speechless as ever, to the trail. In 1894 Daisy gave up. Placing Arnold in a boarding school near his paternal grandparents' home just outside Sydney, she sailed back to England.

She stayed in London for five years, struggling to come to terms with her mistakes, unable to decide between England and Australia and torn between freedom and family. Since her money was all in Australia she was faced with the novelty of having to earn her own living; for three years she worked first as a secretary and then as a journalist on the *Review of Reviews*, one of the leading literary journals of the day, and spent another two years with a publishing company. But her conscience would not leave her in peace; she knew she would eventually have to commit herself one way or the other – and in order to do that she would have to see Jack and Arnold again. So in 1899 she set sail once more for Australia.

Her meeting with her husband and her son was disastrous – in the five years since she had last seen them Jack had become even more morose and slovenly and the graceless little boy had grown into a sullen adolescent. She never blamed Jack for the failure of their marriage – she knew that the fault was as much hers as his – and they were never divorced. They just went their separate ways; Jack back to his job as head stockman on a station in the north, Arnold back to his grandparents in Sydney and Daisy towards her own personal destiny.

★　　　★　　　★　　　★

Just before she had left London a letter had been published in *The Times* alleging cruelty by the white settlers of North-Western Australia towards the local aborigines. Daisy had contacted the editor of *The Times* and offered to carry out a full investigation of the allegations on the newspaper's behalf. Her offer had been accepted – and now she set off to pursue her enquiries.

> Shortly after I landed at Perth I obtained a buggy and horses and camp gear and journeyed by sea to Port Hedland [nearly 1000 miles to the north] . . . I then traversed in my buggy eight hundred miles of country, taking six months to

accomplish it. I could not prove one charge of cruelty except that of 'giving offal to natives instead of good meat' and 'sending them away from the stations without food when work was slack'. . . . So much for the allegations that awakened my interest in the Australian aborigines, and which were the beginning of my life's work among them. *The Times* published the result of my investigations and the matter dropped for a decade.

The assignment did more for Daisy than just help her through a crisis – it gave her life a new direction. The misery of her marriage and her subsequent failure to find fulfilment even in motherhood had left her feeling empty and depressed; her youthful *joie de vivre* had been doused along with her dreams. The disillusioned, sober Daisy that emerged from the trauma had been badly in need of a Cause – and in her encounters with 'the sylvan people, carefree and unclad', it looked as though she might have found one.

On her return to Perth she went to visit Dean Martelli, an Italian Roman Catholic priest who had been her fellow-passenger on the return voyage to Australia and who had proved to be a mine of information about the aborigines. Martelli introduced her to Bishop Gibney, the Roman Catholic Bishop of Western Australia, with whom he was planning a visit to the Trappist Mission at Beagle Bay. Bishop Gibney invited Daisy to accompany them. 'I accepted with alacrity and made my preparations for the journey.'

Beagle Bay was remote even by Australian standards; 2000 miles north round the coast from Perth with another 1000 miles still to go before reaching Darwin. The nearest town was Broome, 250 miles away, and the nearest railway stopped 400 miles to the south. The mission had been founded by Bishop Gibney ten years earlier with the aim of bringing civilisation and Christianity to the aborigine tribes drawn from the interior by the novelties of the coastal pearling stations. For the monks they had been ten years of back-breaking and sometimes heart-breaking struggle; cyclones, sandstorms and bushfires repeatedly demolished their buildings, ruined their crops and killed their animals, and their influence over the aborigines they were there to help remained disappointingly tenuous. But now another threat was hanging over the mission. The Trappists had been warned that they must satisfy the government valuer that they had improved the value of their 10 000-acre holding by £5000 or they would lose their subsidy and the prospect of freehold tenure. The Bishop and the Dean were hurrying to the rescue, and they had a special reason for inviting Daisy to go with him. As a reputable journalist with six months' experience of travelling amongst the aborigines of the north-west, she was in an ideal position to evaluate and then to publicise the work of the mission, thus reinforcing the Trappists' claim for continued government support.

The two elderly Catholic priests and the forty-one-year-old Irish lady left Perth at the end of July 1900 on the ten-day voyage to Broome. There they transferred to the *Sree pas Sair*, an ancient yacht that had once belonged to Rajah Brooke of Sarawak but which now served, stripped of all comforts, as a supply lugger for the off-shore pearling fleets. Three days in this rickety and malodorous vessel took them to the shores of Beagle Bay and Daisy's first sight of the mission; 'a collection of tumbledown, paper-bark monastery cells, a tiny bark chapel and a community room of corrugated iron.'

The little French abbot welcomed Daisy most politely, but her arrival had clearly thrown him into a state of some confusion. The reason was soon revealed – not only was there no accommodation suitable for a woman at the monastery but, according to Trappist rules, no woman except a queen could be allowed inside its walls. A dispensation was needed. Fortunately the Bishop and the Dean were on hand to give it and, reassured, the 'dear little man' admitted Daisy and insisted on placing his own cell at her disposal. 'Perhaps the first woman in history to sleep in a Trappist's bed, I was allotted the abbot's bag bed and seaweed pillow. I awoke to hear the natives singing a Gregorian chant in the little chapel nearby.'

There was no question of this being just a sight-seeing tour for Daisy – in fact she would look back on the four months she spent at Beagle Bay as being 'nothing but the sheerest hard work'. She found herself weeding and hoeing and digging, clearing wells, erecting fences, propagating tomato plants and dandling the babies of the aborigine women who were supposed to be helping her. It took the four resident monks a little time to get used to having a white woman in their midst. But her brisk commonsense allayed their fears that she might fall into a fit of the vapours and her easy friendliness soon convinced them that her presence constituted no threat to their immortal souls. They were quick to appreciate, too, her skill in wheedling a useful contribution out of the incurably lazy aborigine women.

> I worked like a Trojan but the force of my example failed dismally. Day after day those women played with the babies and laughed both with and at me, full of merriment and good feeling. Now and again one of them took up the spade or the hoe in a stirring of conscience, but not for long. I tried to gather the babies and children and play with them to let their mothers do a little manual labour, and I started ring-a-ring-a-roses. No sooner had we got into the swing of the game than every woman and girl downed tools to join in. I compromised. We adults must work, and when the rest-time came at hot midday or evening we would have games. The little plan worked and so we worked and played merrily throughout. As I worked they talked to me and told me a little of their laws.

Although she had the greatest admiration for the practical work of missionaries in general, and of the Trappists at Beagle Bay in particular,

Daisy had less sympathy with their efforts to convert the aborigines to Christianity. An Anglican herself, she felt strongly that proselytisation hindered rather than advanced the aborigines' attempts to come to terms with white culture. But while she remained as their guest she managed to keep tactfully silent on this score.

The final task at the end of four months was to make a survey of the entire 10 000 acres covered by the Beagle Bay lease. Her description of the two-week trudge 'over marsh and through scrub, now lame from the stones and prickles, now up to our thighs in a bog, walking sometimes twelve miles a day in a steamy heat of 106 degrees' concludes with the astonishing information that throughout the whole gruelling exercise she was dressed in corsets, stiff collar, long skirt and high-heeled boots. It was her proud boast that she always 'preserved a scrupulous neatness and all the little trappings and accoutrements of my own very particular mode of dress'. There would be no 'going native' for Mrs Bates: no matter how dirty her task, how hot the sun or how primitive and scantily clad her companions, not once in thirty-five years of living and working in the Australian bush was she tempted to relax her rigid standards of propriety and elegance.

Completion of the survey coincided exactly with the arrival of the official valuer. 'He was surprised to see a thriving property where he had expected ruin and decay. Every screw and post, every animal and plant, was meticulously valued and the sum reached was over £6000. The mission was saved for the natives.' Daisy's last task at Beagle Bay was to lay the foundation stone for a new convent and monastery.

*　　　*　　　*　　　*

Delighted with their success, the Bishop and the Dean packed up for their return to Perth. Then Daisy announced that she was not going with them.

In the cities and along the settled stretches of the coast, seventy or eighty years of contact with the white man had already done catastrophic and irreparable damage to the traditional lives of the aborigines. But there were vast areas of the interior that no white man had ever penetrated and where the aborigines still lived as they had done for countless generations. The months Daisy had spent on the fringe of this as yet unsullied land had given her 'a few stray glimpses of the strange hidden life of this last remnant of palaeolithic man'. Now she had decided to stay on in the north-west and embark on a systematic study of aboriginal beliefs and customs while they still survived. This decision would set the pattern for the rest of her life.

The next eight months were spent among the Koolarrabulloo tribes of Broome, and it was there that my first attempts were rewarded. By the wells and the creeks, sitting in the camps in the firelight, on horse-back and on foot my notebook and pencil were always with me. I would camp out sometimes for days, sharing my food, nursing the babies, gathering vegetable food with the women and making friends with the old men. Thus I extended and verified my knowledge by gradual degrees until I gained a unique insight into the whole northern aboriginal social system, and its life-story from babyhood to age. Every moment of my spare time was given to this self-imposed and fascinating study.

Daisy attributed her almost uncanny affinity with the aborigines to the fact that she was Irish. There was so much that the aborigine nature had in common with the Celt – both races were emotional, quick-tempered, fatalistic and superstitious; they shared a deep attachment to the legends and folk-tales of their ancestors, and a haunting undercurrent of melancholy ran through the songs and stories of Irish peasant and Australian aboriginal alike. It seemed but a short step from the leprechauns and the little people of County Tipperary to the *Nalja*, the spirit of an old man with white hair whose voice issued from his armpits, and the *ngargalulla*, or dream-babies, of north-western Australia.

This instinctive understanding of their symbolism and mythology, and her limitless patience, eventually led to the aborigines accepting Daisy as a kindred spirit. 'At the men's hidden corroborees, far from my own people in the heart of the bush, because I showed no quiver of timidity, or of revulsion of feeling, or of levity, because I was thinking with my "black man's mind", I have never been a stranger.' The first and most fundamental lesson that she learned was not to measure the aborigine by any standards except his own – he was a unique being, shy, private and peaceable, who took the line of least resistance in his dealings with the white man and answered leading questions as he thought was expected of him, regardless of the truth. 'Only when you are part of the landscape that he knows and loves will he accord you the compliment of living his normal life and taking no notice of you.' She learned to speak the native language – 'a series of vocal gymnastics quite impossible to the average white linguist and which, I am perfectly sure, in all my years of juggling with them, have altered the form of my larynx' – and she pretended that her native name was 'Kallower' (meaning Grandmother) and that she was a *mirruroo-jando*, or 'magic woman' who had been one of the twenty-two wives of Leeberr, a patriarchal or 'dreamtime' father. 'After that the way was clear.'

She quickly grew to appreciate the natural harmony of the aborigines' finely balanced relationship with their environment, and the more she learned the better she understood the tragedy that had already befallen their coastal cousins and which, sooner or later, would overwhelm them all. The white man's invasion had crashed through their gentle dreaming world, shattering the centuries-old structure of their lives, undermining their beliefs, pouring scorn on their heritage and leaving them wandering like lost ghosts in a sandy limbo, unable either to cling to the past or come to terms with the future.

Her appreciation was never sentimental; she did not try to romanticise or glamorise the aborigine and made no attempt to gloss over the darker side of his character. She described even the most abhorrent of his practices in meticulous detail – the often brutal treatment of women by the men who were their absolute masters, and the cannibalism, particularly of 'baby-meat' and the flesh of their enemies, which was apparently common throughout the continent. She made no attempt to justify these excesses – but she did try to understand them, for they were part and parcel of the aborigine's life.

She followed her eight-month sojourn with the unspoiled Koolarra-bulloo of the north-west with two years among the already benighted Bubbulmun of the south-west. Travelling sometimes by train but mostly by horse-drawn buggy, she roamed the coastal plains around Perth and the lush forested slopes of the Darling Ranges, and her forebodings were justified at every turn. Everywhere she went she met the straggling remnants of dispossessed tribes; sitting down with them in the bush she listened as they struggled to articulate their misery. And she saw to her horror that even those who had managed to evade the white man's diseases – measles, whooping cough, influenza and syphilis – were dying sometimes from sheer heartsick despair.

She was too loyal and too patriotic to condemn the white man for taking over – his fault, as she saw it, lay merely in his inability to understand the devastating effects of his ways.

> The pioneers of Western Australia were noble men and women and nearly all of them were above reproach and more than kindly in their treatment of the aboriginal. But it was a kindness that killed as surely and as swiftly as cruelty would have done. The Australian native can withstand all the reverses of nature, fiendish droughts and sweeping floods, horrors of thirst and enforced starvation, but he cannot withstand civilisation.

The white man was not always so generous in return. Although liberals would appreciate her endeavours and acknowledge her expertise, there were many others who raised pained eyebrows at her association with 'natives' and dismissed her contemptuously as 'the woman who lives with the blacks'.

*　　*　　*　　*

During her wanderings in the south-west she contributed regular articles to the Australian scientific press and by the time she returned to Perth in 1904 her reputation as an 'authority on all things aboriginal' was firmly established. Her response to being given such an extravagant label was gently remonstrative; '. . . the riddle of the native mind is the study, not of a year or two of field work, but of a whole lifetime'; but she was happy to accept the official recognition that followed. The Registrar-General of Western Australia, Malcolm Fraser, had been planning for some time to compile an official record of the customs and dialects of the aborigines. An enlightened and humane administrator, Fraser would have undertaken the task himself had he had the time and the necessary expertise. But since he had neither he was looking for someone who had both – and at his suggestion Daisy applied to the Department of Aboriginal Affairs (the DAA) for the job of Official Recorder. She was instantly accepted.

For a year she lived and worked in Perth, collecting and collating reports and information on the aborigines from all over Australia. She also started writing up the copious notes she had taken during her wanderings and continued the compilation of the dictionary of aborigine words and phrases that she had started at Broome. In 1905 she set up her first real camp in the Maamba Reserve at Cannington, now a suburb of Perth but then still 'a beautiful kingdom of bush, rich in native foods and fruits'.

> A circular tent, 14ft in diameter, sagging about me in the wet and ballooning in the wind, was my home for two years in that little patch of bushland bright with wild flowers. There by a camp fire I would be on duty from night until morning, collecting scraps of language, old legends, old customs, trying to conjure a nation of the past from these few and homeless derelicts, always in haste, as they died about me one by one, in fear lest I should be too late.

Although she was still pessimistic about the fate of the aborigines, she had not yet given up hope of being able to protect them – particularly now that her efforts on their behalf had government backing.

Certainly her research and her opinions were increasingly winning the respect of scientists, ethnologists and anthropologists. By 1910 she had compiled an 800-page treatise on the strength of which she was appointed a Fellow of the Anthropological Society of Australasia, an Honorary Correspondent of the Royal Anthropological Society of Great Britain and Ireland and a Member of the Royal Geographical Society of Melbourne. Fraser was so impressed with her manuscript that he suggested she send it to Dr Andrew Lang, a distinguished anthropologist in London, who would revise it for publication in book form. The manuscript was duly despatched – but Daisy's mind was on other things. For some time now she had been having serious doubts about her official position. She had accepted her job as recorder in the belief that she and her employers were working for a common aim, but it was becoming increasingly obvious to her that they were not.

Official policy towards aborigines was geared towards their rapid and total integration with the white community. In order to survive, the aborigine must adopt the white man's laws and his religion, his morals and his medicine. If a few unfortunates were trampled in the rush then that was the price of the survival of their species – the occasional tragedy was inevitable, but the end fully justified the means.

Daisy's view was exactly the opposite. If the aborigines were to survive they must be left alone. They must be allowed to live as they had always lived, wild, naked and free, as far away as possible from the corrupting influences of white civilisation.

So troubled was she by this dichotomy that, had it not been for the arrival in Perth of an anthropological study group from Cambridge University, she might have seriously considered handing in her resignation. But the anthropologists, Professor Radcliffe-Brown and Mr Grant Watson, were in Western Australia to undertake field work among the aborigines of the interior and they were looking for someone with first-hand knowledge of the aborigines to act as their liaison officer and translator. Daisy was the obvious choice.

She had great hopes of the expedition. It would give her an opportunity to share her knowledge with other anthropologists and to learn from them in turn. She would also be able to fill in some of the gaps in her research. But it did not quite work out that way.

The expedition's base camp was set up just outside the little town of Sandstone 400 miles north-east of Perth. Among the hundred or so natives from the surrounding districts that gathered to stare at the new arrivals Daisy met several old friends and, to paraphrase Gertrude Bell, 'was soon deep in the gossip of the bush'. She talked to them of old times and mutual acquaintances and took a group of them to look for honey ants, a great local delicacy. She could not resist offering their catch to Mr Grant Watson for his supper, knowing the very idea would turn his cultivated stomach and was wickedly pleased when it did. Just as Watson and Radcliffe-Brown were beginning to make a little headway in their anthropological discussions with the aborigines, the whole group suddenly scattered. One returned just long enough to tell Daisy that a policeman was coming with a 'big mob' before taking to his heels and fleeing into the bush. The 'big mob' turned out to be the police constable from Sandstone and some of his men on an official inspection.

Acting in their capacity as Protectors of Aborigines, police officers were authorised to examine women as well as men – any who were infected with either venereal disease or tuberculosis were immediately moved to isolation hospitals. Their methods were frequently insensitive and sometimes downright rough; and Daisy watched, shocked and appalled, as her friends were subjected to this humiliating ordeal.

> With Professor Radcliffe-Brown's assistance, Grey made his examinations, collected several men and women and drove them away in his cart to Sandstone. I shall never forget the anguish and despair on their faces. The poor decrepit creatures were leaving their land for a destination unknown, a fate they could not understand, and their woe was pitiful. So turbulent and so distressed were all the inhabitants of all the camps in the vicinity that it was useless for us to remain longer.

This incident marked the watershed in Daisy's relationship with the DAA and the start of what would be a thirty-year feud with officialdom. She protested loudly and vigorously to the police, to the DAA and to the press against the outrage. But she did not immediately desert the Cambridge expedition. Professor Radcliffe-Brown decided that the isolation hospitals would make an ideal alternative field for his studies. Bracing herself for the horrors she knew were in store, and fortified by the hope that she might be able to comfort her old friends in their misery, she agreed to go with him. The expedition packed up and followed the stricken natives to the isolation hospitals on Dorré and Bernier Islands off the coast of Western Australia at Caernarvon.

Daisy's description of the conditions in which the aborigines were kept on Dorré and Bernier is as harrowing to read as Kate Marsden's description of the conditions of the lepers in Siberia. Although the sick aborigines were not subjected to the same mindless cruelty as were the lepers, the physical and mental tortures they endured were just as painful and their isolation every bit as devastating.

> When I landed on Bernier island in November 1910 there were only fifteen men left alive there, but I counted thirty-eight graves. On Dorré, where the women were segregated, there were seventy-seven women, many of them bed-ridden. I dared not count the graves. Most of them were in the last stages of venereal disease and tuberculosis. Nothing could save them, yet they had been transported, some of them thousands of miles, to strange and unnatural surroundings and solitude. They were afraid of the hospital, its ceaseless probings and dressings and injections were a daily torture. They were afraid of each other. They were afraid of the ever-moaning sea. The hospital was well kept and the medical work excellently performed, but the natives accepted all the care with a frightful fatalism. They believed that they had been brought here to die, what did it matter if the white man had decided to cut them to pieces first? Through unaccustomed hot baths their withered, sensitive skins, which are never

cleansed in their natural state save by grease and fresh air, became like tissue-paper and parted horribly from the flesh. Some of them cried all day and all night in a listless and terrible monotony of grief. There was no ray of brightness, no gleam of hope.

The expedition remained on the islands for six months while Radcliffe-Brown and Watson studied the effects of various forms of treatment on the natives. Daisy stayed with them, translating, interpreting, helping them write up their notes and, between official duties, caring for the people she now regarded as her children. She knew that although they welcomed the blankets and sweets she provided for them and drew some comfort from her solicitude, what they needed above all else was contact with their families and friends. So she set up a primitive postal service which provided the sick and the dying with a precious link with their own kind. Every time she visited the mainland she would carry a bundle of *bamburu*, little pieces of wood marked with the crude scratches that served the aborigines as an informal sign language, and arrange for them to be delivered to their destinations. 'To watch the poor fellows in their fatal lassitude trying to mark the *bamburu* they wanted to send to their women, was a pitiful sight, but to see the joy on their faces when I returned with *bamburu* from the absent loved ones was heartrending.'

The isolation hospitals on Dorré and Bernier were closed down and the islands abandoned not long after Daisy left, but her experiences there would haunt her for the rest of her life. And it was from the patients there that she earned her final name.

> To the grey-headed, and the grey-bearded, men and women and children alike, I had been known for many years as *kallower*, a grandmother but a spurious and very young one. Here in Dorré I became *kabbarli*, Grandmother to the sick and dying, and *kabbarli* I was to remain in all my wanderings.

*   *   *   *

The expedition was wound up in the middle of 1911 and Daisy returned to Perth to discuss her future with Malcolm Fraser. He understood and respected her objections to official policy regarding the aborigines, but advised her to stay with the DAA and work towards her goals from within. A vacancy had occurred for a Chief Protector of Aborigines for the Northern Territories – and although the position was not within his gift, he wrote her a glowing reference.

Despite his enthusiastic support, and that of her old friend Bishop Gibney, she did not get the job. The official reason given was that as a woman she would be subjected to too many risks and would need a police escort to travel amongst the aborigines. To one who had lived entirely alone and unprotected amongst the aborigines for years without coming to the slightest harm, this explanation sounded hollow indeed. Daisy was convinced the real reason was that the DAA had taken exception to her outspoken criticisms of its working methods. But there was nothing she could do. With as much grace as she could muster she accepted the DAA's alternative suggestion – that she should go as honorary protector (and therefore unpaid) to the Eucla district. She arrived in November 1912.

Even in Daisy's day Eucla was nothing but a name on the map, 'a street of ruined houses almost completely engulfed in the sand just at the point where the majestic cliffs of the Great Australian Bight recede inland to form the western edge of the vast Nullarbor Plain'. The town had been built to house workers on the transcontinental telegraph line and their families, but when the line had been completed and automatic operating systems had taken over, the town was abandoned. The aborigines of the surrounding area, whose lives and lands had been disrupted by the initial influx, had drifted in and out of the settlement, scrounging off and being exploited by its inhabitants. By the time the town was evacuated, their self-reliance and self-respect had trickled away to evaporate in the burning sands. They were left derelict.

Since she was no longer being paid by anyone Daisy felt free to work for and with the aborigines on her own terms. She pitched her tent two miles from the settlement near the beach, from where she could watch the 'great sweeping billows of the Southern Ocean rolling in like thunder, sometimes a single wave two miles long'. And she stayed there for two years.

Her little tent became a beacon to the wandering groups of aborigines uprooted from their traditional lands by the remorseless march of the white man's progress. From north and west, from the coastal plains and the far hills, they drifted in to sit with *kabbarli*, their dreamtime grandmother, to talk of times gone by, to tell their stories, act out their rituals and, as Daisy saw it, to wait for death. When she arrived at Eucla there were thirty or so aborigines in the area – by the time she left there would be more than a hundred and fifty.

Nothing had come of her planned book – Lang had died before finishing his revisions and the manuscript was languishing somewhere in England – but her old habits were hard to break. Every day she wrote up her notes. Every story she was told, every new dialect she heard spoken, every scrap of new information was meticulously written down. She described the rituals and ceremonies that attended conception, birth, the onset of puberty, marriage and death, she translated and recorded legends, songs and folk tales and she constructed detailed tables of inter-tribal relationships. She corresponded, too, with her friends from the scientific and anthropological worlds, many of whom expressed their dismay that she should bury herself in the back of beyond and begged her to return to civilisation. Their pleas were easy to resist.

> I made the decision to dedicate the rest of my life to this fascinating study. I admit that it was scarcely a sacrifice. Apart from the joy of the work for its own sake, the freshness, the freedom, the farness meant much more to me now than the life of cities.

Psychologists would probably have some explanation for Daisy's self-imposed exile. 'Socially inadequate', maybe, or 'suffering from repressed guilt over the failure of her marriage and neglect of her son'. Searching through her writings, however, there is no sign of any inner torment or psychological complexity. As far as she was concerned it was all very straightforward – she had become interested in the aborigines in her professional capacity as a journalist; their undocumented lives had presented a fascinating challenge to her enquiring mind and now she was too involved to withdraw.

> By this time I was a confirmed wanderer, a nomad even as the aborigines. So close had I been in contact with them that it was now impossible for me to relinquish the work. So savage and so simple, so much astray and so utterly helpless were they, that somehow they became my responsibility.

*　　　*　　　*　　　*

In mid-1914 came an invitation that Daisy could not resist; she was asked to address the congress of the British Association for the Advancement of Science at Adelaide, Melbourne and Sydney. Relishing the prospect of some intellectual stimulation, she borrowed a camel-buggy, drove herself the 450 miles to Yalata and took ship for Adelaide. But the 'happy and exhilarating experience' of the congress was somewhat offset by the startling discovery that Europe was at war and the whole world was in turmoil. 'My own thought had been so remote from international concerns for so long that I stood aghast at the news.'

The congress was a great success, Daisy's papers were received enthusiastically by her learned audience and she spent the succeeding month lecturing in Adelaide. In September a petition signed by many of the delegates as well as by representatives of what she rather vaguely called 'women's organisations' was presented to Sir Richard Butler, Minister in control of the Department for Aborigine Affairs, that Daisy be appointed Protector of Aborigines for South Australia. But Daisy had no reason to suppose her two-year absence would have changed anything, so instead of waiting to hear the result of his deliberations, she returned to Eucla.

The decision was never made. The war had given Australians something new to worry about; by the beginning of 1915 their sons were fighting and dying on the other side of the world – and in the face of that horror even the staunchest of her supporters found it hard to concentrate on the fate of the aborigines.

*　　*　　*　　*

Daisy stayed in Eucla for the duration of the war, returning to Adelaide in 1918 only because her health broke down. When her 'vigour was restored' she spent several months in charge of a convalescent home for wounded soldiers – a job for which she considered her only qualification to be years of experience 'mothering' the aborigines; it was the only time in her life that she had white patients in her care. Although her conscience told her she should not grudge one minute of the time she spent looking after 'these brave boys', she found it hard to settle in the city, and her mind constantly strayed out into the bush where her 'grandchildren' were facing a new misery – the arrival of the Trans-Australia Railway. A few weeks before her sixtieth birthday she decided she could bear it no longer. Bidding adieu to her friends she packed her bags and set off once more into the bush.

> When I came to Ooldea siding in September 1919 I found conditions difficult. The newly formed railway settlements had not yet settled down after the chaos of the very recent construction. Aftermath of war was still in the air and the unrest among the white communities was almost as distressing as the obvious degeneration of the black.

Ooldea came to symbolise for Daisy the fateful and one-sided conflict between new and old Australia. 'Nothing more than one of the many depressions in the never-ending sandhills, Ooldea is one of nature's miracles. No white man coming to this place would ever guess that that dreary hollow with the sand blowing across it was an unfailing fountain, yet a mere scratch and the magic waters welled in sight.' Even during the worst years of drought the underground reservoir at Ooldea had never failed, and for centuries aborigine tribes from hundreds of miles around had gathered beside this wondrous water to perform their ceremonies and rituals.

Yet somehow the white man had discovered it. And he had seen no signposts by the dreary hollow saying *PRIVATE*, no fences or boundary markers or any of the other accepted symbols of ownership. So he had commandeered the waters of the unfailing fountain for the locomotives of his new railway; he had run the gleaming tracks for his thundering 'serpent-devil' across the traditional gathering ground; and he had decided, in his goodness, to allow the black man access to his precious water from taps in the siding yard.

Daisy arrived in Ooldea to find the whole area littered with the victims of this cultural collision. Deprived of their inherited ownership, aborigines from all over the south and west of Australia were straggling along the line in increasing numbers. Travelling westwards several years later, journalist Ernestine Hill would be horrified to see 'old women in reeking rags, young mothers with babies dragging at their breasts, naked children, skin and bone with matted hair, their sad, cavernous eyes a nest of flies, . . . silent, pitiful little groups and families, knowing not a word of English', begging for scraps from the dining cars and being stared at and photographed by prurient passengers who threw them pennies for their pains.

'They [the aborigines] do not know that they are bringing about their own annihilation,' mourned Daisy, 'they think that the train and its people will go away and leave them the things to play with.' The only possessions which the men could barter for food and alcohol and the trashy trappings of white civilisation were their boomerangs, their spears, and their women. 'Prostitution was rife, and many unfortunates had already reaped the wages of sin. When the first half-caste babies appeared, the wild mothers believed that they were the results of eating white man's food and rubbed them frantically with charcoal to restore their black health and colour, till often they died.' Venereal disease was rife too, and measles and influenza and crime, and abject, untold misery.

To the passing travellers the aborigines looked like the very dregs of humanity. But to Daisy they were her family. There were even, among the unhappy hordes, several familiar faces from her earlier, happier travels, and they fell on their beloved *kabbarli* with cries of joy and begged her to stay with them. Thus it was that she pitched the tent and set up the camp that was to be her home for the next sixteen years.

> Outside my little tent the natives would come to await my attention, old friends sitting patiently and naked newcomers shyly flitting about among the scrub, sometimes two days before they summoned courage to approach this Kabbarli of whom they had heard so far away. They came to me from the Mann, the Gosse, the Everard, the Peterman and the Musgrave ranges and from far across the north-western borders of the state. . . . zigzagging in the desert for food and water they followed the tracks of those who had come before them, disintegrating, reuniting, mourning and rejoicing, and every moon fleeing further from their hereditary waters. At last the remnants arrived on the rim of civilisation outside my windbreak. All along the thousand miles of the railway there was no other sanctuary, no half-way house between the white men's traffic and the native intelligence five thousand years behind. My first task, as the groups stepped over the threshold of civilisation, was to set them at ease and clothe them, learn their names and their homes, explain the white man's laws and tell them of the resources and the dangers of this new age they had stumbled into.

The sixteen years Daisy spent at Ooldea were 'years of so much increasing difficulty and disheartenment that had it not been for the guiding light of my ideals of service, and my deep love and sympathy for the natives, I could never have lived them through.' After the first year she decided that the siding, in full view of the trains, was not the best place to carry on her work for the natives and she moved to a sandy gully two miles to the north. But a series of disasters, both natural and man-made, threatened to overwhelm her 'little household'. An eight-week railway strike cut off her only food supply and reduced her diet to one plate of cold porridge a day. An epidemic of measles had her single-handedly nursing seventeen patients simultaneously in their makeshift shelters. In 1922 she caught an eye infection from one of her patients which resulted for a time in almost total blindness – 'not once but several times, bending over my fireplace to make my cup of tea, a smell of burning was my only warning that my clothing was on fire' – and her 1000-mile journey to consult an oculist in Perth was her only holiday, 'if holiday it can be called', in twelve years. In 1926 careless over-exploitation by the railway company resulted in terminal pollution of the subterranean reservoir; the water from her own supply was rendered undrinkable and Daisy, now sixty-eight years old, had to carry every drop of drinking water two miles across the sands. But the ultimate ordeal was a devastating drought, 'perhaps the worst in South Australian history'. No measurable rain fell on Ooldea for eight years. Even the native foods – fruits, roots and berries – shrivelled and died; fierce hot winds lashed her camp and threatened to blow away her tent, daytime temperatures rose to a record 126°F and daily sandstorms buried her bed, her table and her typewriter under deep drifts.

But there were high spots too. In 1920 she was appointed a Justice of the Peace for South Australia and later the same year she was asked to arrange for the aborigines to hold a corroboree in honour of the Prince of Wales, later and briefly King Edward VIII, whose train was to pass through Ooldea on his tour of Australia. 'His Royal Highness remained for two and a half hours, and was intensely interested throughout.' But mostly it was a downward spiral of sickness and sorrow.

Her many friends in the worlds of anthropology and journalism took up her cause, pleading for government funding for her work and putting her name forward every time a post of Protector of Aborigines fell vacant. But the DAA had still not forgiven her for her public denunciation of their policies. Not only did they refuse to consider her for the job of Official Protector, but not once during the whole time she was at Ooldea did they grant her any funds towards her work. So she used her own money to provide the natives with food, clothing and medicine. She had already sold the property in Western Australia that she had bought all those years before in an attempt to get Jack to settle down. The proceeds had soon been engulfed in 'the usual routine order of flour, tea, sugar, onions, medical supplies, dress material, shirts, trousers and a little tobacco for comfort'. In 1924 she sold the little plot of land she had bought outside Perth on which she planned to build a home for her declining years, and gradually thereafter she sold almost all her possessions, 'including my side-saddle and bridle – last relics of a happy past.' When her entire inheritance was gone, she swallowed her pride and wrote to her friends pleading for donations; and she supplemented their generosity by 'contributing to Australian and Home [i.e. English] newspapers my scientific gleanings'.

* * * *

By the time the great drought broke Daisy was seventy years old. But if her blue eyes were dimmed by years of searing light and her weatherbeaten complexion bore the unmistakeable brown blotches of age, her figure was as spry as ever and her daily toilet just as fastidious. Every morning at sunrise the flap of her eight-foot by ten-foot tent would open and the meticulous little lady would emerge dressed 'according to the simple but exact dictates of fashion as I left it, when Victoria was Queen'.

In 1932 she received a visit that would turn her, for a while, into a celebrity. Ernestine Hill, an internationally successful Australian journalist, had heard about this eccentric old lady who had chosen to live among the aborigines, and arrived on the train with the scent of a good story in her nostrils. The two women liked each other on sight. Daisy was so delighted to have a visitor who spoke her language and understood her work that for two days she hardly drew breath. Ernestine for her part was in turns moved, overawed, horrified, intrigued and amazed by Daisy and her little world. In a personal memoir written more than twenty years after Daisy's death she would recall her as 'independent to a fault, quick to take offence, easily prejudiced, withering in scorn, but always a model of good form. . . her chief charm was her voice, gentle and low, with an Irish intonation but not a shadow of a brogue.'

Although she did not agree with Daisy's perception of the aborigines as a doomed race, and would look back on her efforts to keep black and white Australians apart with the eye of one familiar with the modern concept of 'apartheid', Ernestine could see that there was no suggestion in Daisy's mind of white superiority, and could appreciate that she was motivated entirely by her deep love, respect and understanding of the aborigines. Ernestine's subsequent articles were widely syndicated and soon all Australia was talking about 'the charming little lady of the old school, daughter of the sporting gentry of Ireland who was accepted as a tribes-woman and guardian spirit of the most occult race in the world'.

But Ernestine had been alarmed by her visit. Daisy had admitted to her that 'a potato in the ashes, now and again a spoonful of rice that nine times out of ten was burned in my absence or absent-mindedness, occasionally the treat of a boiled egg, and always tea, my panacea for all ills, were the full extent of my culinary craft.' The middle of the Nullarbor Plain, 400 miles from the nearest doctor, was no place for a forgetful, partially sighted septuagenarian who had never learned to cook and who was so busy looking after her beloved aborigines that she was seriously neglecting her own health. Daisy's physical frailty had Ernestine racking her brains for a way of enticing her out of the wilderness. But there was no need. In August 1933 she received an excited letter from Daisy telling her that she was on her way to Canberra. A series of pitched battles between settlers and natives in the Northern Territory had led the Minister of the Interior to send an urgent telegram to Ooldea inviting advice.

Daisy caught the next train to Adelaide, and two days later was enjoying the first proper bath she had taken for twelve years. The sudden return to civilisation, though, was a shock. 'Gone were the Australia and the Australians I had known. In my brief and hurried glimpse of the now mature and graceful cities of Adelaide and Melbourne, quite alone and in my old-world garb, I felt a stranger and an anachronism.' In Canberra she was introduced to the Prime Minister and most of his Cabinet, and was gratified by the respect and attention she received from the various Ministers of State. Her visit lasted for three months; all the luxuries and amenities of life that she had lacked for so long were at her disposal, and she relished 'the pleasant intellectual association' of her own kind. But her solution to the troubles in the north – that she should travel there herself to mediate – was turned down on the grounds that she was too old to make the journey.

Although the government had a point, Daisy obviously did not see it that way. As far as she was concerned it was just the same old story. She returned to the Nullarbor, dejected and disappointed – only to find that in her absence a new government camp had been set up at Ooldea by two missionaries. They were in the process of building a church and were already providing meals and shelter for all Daisy's old friends. The government had stolen her aborigines. Her battle was lost.

Her only consolation came in a telegram shortly after New Year 1934: she had been awarded the CBE. 'This recognition from our beloved Sovereign, coming as it did when my little camp was almost empty of provender and my heart of hope, has been the full reward of my life's service.'

*　　　*　　　*　　　*

Once again Ernestine Hill came to the rescue. She knew that Daisy had taken voluminous notes throughout her long years at Ooldea. Now she suggested that she owed it to her aboriginal friends to write a book incorporating everything she had learned about their customs and their way of life. Such a book would ensure that, even if they themselves were doomed to die, their story would not. It was a shrewd suggestion, and probably the only way of stopping Daisy from sitting quietly down in the desert in the aboriginal fashion and waiting for death. In 1934 she packed her bags and prepared to leave Ooldea.

> I had passed the allotted span of my life by five long years. My step was as light and my heart as gay as they had been in youth, but I could no longer shut my eyes to the fact that if I were to accomplish my work for Australia and its lost people, I must lose no time. The hope was qualified with regret, for now I must bid farewell to that little tent home patched with a hundred patches, ragged and empty and devoid of comfort, yet so full of loving memories; Kabbarli must take leave of her grandchildren.

Looking back over the sixteen years she had lived at Ooldea, Daisy would decide that her greatest achievement was the fact that no more half-caste children had been born in the vicinity since she arrived. Her bitterest disappointment was that amongst the hundreds of aborigines who 'sat down' with her at Ooldea, 'there was not one that ever returned to his own waters and the natural bush life.'

She wrote her book. She also collated and filed her notes and donated them, ninety-four folios in all, to Australia's National Library. But she still could not settle in civilisation. In 1941 she decided to return to her wilderness and at the age of eighty made herself a new camp, east of Ooldea. For a year she waited patiently for her 'grandchildren' to come and 'sit down' with her once more. None ever came. Despite her efforts they had drifted on, past the warnings she had tried to give them, over the barriers she had tried to build round them, through the gates she had tried to close in front of them, and into the very world she had left for their sakes. The same words used so often to describe them – 'sad', 'displaced', 'anachronistic' – apply with a desperate poignancy to her own final years.

The 'confirmed wanderer', the 'nomad even as the aborigines', died in 1951 in an old people's home in Adelaide. She was ninety-one.

CHAPTER SEVEN

'A TOUCHING & SYMPATHETIC FIGURE'
· Alexandra David-Neel ·

N o two ladies better illustrate the diversity of characters in this collection than Alexandra David-Neel and Amelia Edwards. Amelia's world resembled a suburban garden planted with all the Victorian virtues; trim clumps of Convention and Etiquette, formal rows of Good Breeding, Personal Elegance and Decorum, immaculate paths paved with Propriety – and the whole bounded by a high, prickly hedge of Social Taboos. Alexandra's world was boundless – not for her the confines of suburbia or the reassuring security of a garden. Rather she chose to wander the wilderness, to tramp the heights, 'to dream of high hills, immense deserted steppes and impassable landscapes of glaciers'.

Miss Edwards made a virtue out of 'drifting to Egypt by accident'. By the time Madame David-Neel set out on her journey to Lhasa she was completely fluent in the Tibetan language, she was a practising Buddhist and had been delving into the customs, literature, folklore and legends of the country for more than twelve years. Where Amelia's travelling equipment comprised several trunkloads of clothes, shoes, sun hats and parasols, a small reference library, sketching materials, notebooks, mosquito curtains, medical supplies and other such essential paraphernalia, Alexandra's wardrobe consisted of the clothes she was wearing and her entire baggage would not have filled Amelia's picnic basket.

Both ladies were writers and both would write books about their respective journeys. But while Amelia's *A Thousand Miles Up the Nile* is a model of its kind, Alexandra's *My Journey to Lhasa* is an uneasy travelogue. Some of those unfamiliar with her life and philosophy have attributed this to the fact that it was written in English by a Frenchwoman; others have decided that it was because she was making most of it up. But the real reason for its awkwardness is that Alexandra herself was uncomfortable with the accepted formula and no admirer of the genre. Of the sixteen or seventeen books that she would write during her long life, this one is both the best-known and the one that does the least justice to her extraordinary talents.

Although her reputation today rests largely on the fact that she was the first western woman to reach the Forbidden City, as far as she was concerned her journey to Lhasa was a diversion. She went to Lhasa, specifically, because she had been told not to. Having done so, having proved her point, she could not resist rubbing it in by publishing an account of her journey in a form that would ensure its widest possible readership. And since it was the British who had forbidden her in the first place, how sweet to be able to write of her triumph in their language. In her introduction to the book she goes out of her way to stress that she had nothing but friendly feelings towards the English nation as a whole; she supposed that 'the citizens of Great Britain and the Dominions are as little acquainted with the devious proceedings of political officers regarding far-off colonies or protectorates, as is the rest of the world.'

The 'devious' political officer in question was Charles Bell, the British Resident at Gangtok in Sikkim. Having got wind of Alexandra's presence on and indeed over the Tibetan border in 1915 he had written an angry letter ordering her to leave Tibetan soil. Her immediate and indignant reaction was to ask 'What right had they [the British] to erect barriers round a country that was not even lawfully theirs? If Heaven is the Lord's, the earth is the inheritance of man and any honest traveller has the right to walk as he chooses all over the globe that is his.' She had crossed the border into Tibet to visit the great monastery at Tashilunpo, home of the Tashi, or Panchen, Lama. After several days spent in delightful discussion with His Holiness and an excursion to the nearby printing works, she was preparing to leave Tibet anyway, so she had complied with Bell's order. But she had also taken a vow, not just to return, but to travel right into the very heart of the country. 'I took an oath that in spite of all obstacles I would reach Lhasa and show what the will of a woman could achieve.'

* * * *

Louise Eugénie Alexandrine Marie David was the only child of a middle-class Belgian mother and a French father. Their marriage was not a happy one and Alexandra's lonely and restricted childhood in Paris turned her into a self-contained, dreamy adolescent with a talent for music, a decided preference for solitude, and a passion for 'The Unknown'.

Raised as a Catholic, she would retain a fascination for religious ritual and ceremony all her life, but in her late teens she renounced Roman Catholicism itself as being too tyrannical and oppressive. As a music student in Paris in the 1880s she was introduced to theosophy, the new philosophy-cum-religion which had arrived in the French capital on the current wave of enthusiasm for all things oriental. Although there is no record of Alexandra ever calling herself a theosophist, there can be no doubt that her early links with the Theosophical Society had a profound effect on her life.

The Society had three declared objects; 'to form a nucleus of the Universal Brotherhood of Humanity, without distinction of race, creed, sex, caste or colour'; 'to encourage the study of comparative religions, philosophy and science'; and 'to investigate unexplained laws of nature and the powers latent in man'. In one form or another, and very much under her own terms, Alexandra would be true to these aims for the next eighty years. She despised politics and condemned colonialism as tantamount to slavery. Although she found the study of science less to her liking, she gladly embraced the study of comparative religions and philosophy. But it was the 'unexplained laws of nature' that she found most intriguing of all – and it was her exploration of mysticism and the occult that would set her apart from other orientalists and equip her so well for her subsequent wanderings in Tibet.

A small inheritance from a godmother allowed her to travel to India and Ceylon in the early 1890s and it was during this trip that her interest in comparative religions became focused on Buddhism. Hélène Blavatsky, the founder of the Theosophical Society, had recently returned from a year-long sojourn at the feet of her 'guru' in Shigatse in southern Tibet, and it was when Alexandra visited the headquarters of the Theosophical Society in Madras that she first heard talk of this 'mysterious land of hidden forces, this country of high summits where the Indians believe their Gods to dwell'.

After a second visit to the East in 1896, when she toured French Indo-China as *première chanteuse* with a Parisian opera company, she abandoned her musical career and enrolled at the Sorbonne to study Sanskrit and Tibetan literature, financing her studies by contributing articles on oriental matters to a variety of learned journals. In 1904, when she was thirty-six years old, she met and very soon afterwards married a distant cousin, Philippe Neel, who was Chief Engineer of Tunis Railways. It took her only a few days to decide that marriage was a mistake and the two – apparently amicably – went their separate ways. Despite the fact that Philippe would remain her loyal correspondent, friend and adviser for the next forty years, financing her travels and acting as her literary agent, Alexandra never mentioned him in any of her books. It was almost as if she was afraid to admit his existence for fear of undermining her own, and the world's, faith in her self-reliance. In 1909 she was offered a post as lecturer in comparative religion at a Belgian university, and at the end of 1910 she was commissioned by the French Ministry of Education to 'make some Oriental researches', including, if possible, an interview with the Dalai Lama.

She left Paris for India early in 1911, expecting her visit to last at the most for a few months. It lasted for fourteen years. The interview she obtained with the Dalai Lama was a revelation. Travelling to his exiled court near Darjeeling Alexandra had her first glimpse of the dark wooded hills and mighty snow-covered peaks that were the Himalayas. 'Here was truly a land different from all others; what an unforgettable vision.' The royal household too seemed like something out of her dreams. The monks who formed the entourage of the Tibetan God-King were serene and courteous; they wore shining yellow satin, dark red cloth and gold brocade and 'related fantastic stories and spoke of a wonderland'. The solemn, neatly-dressed Parisian academic had listened spellbound as the words of the gentle lamas breathed life into her dry, theoretical studies – here was real Buddhism, profound, vibrant, and limitless. 'At last I had found the calm solitude of which I had dreamt since my infancy. After a tiring, cheerless pilgrimage I could see my home.'

His Holiness was surprised and impressed by Alexandra's knowledge and understanding of Buddhist doctrine – rare in any westerner, unique in a western woman. He suggested that she would be able to reach a deeper appreciation of 'Lamaism', or Tibetan Buddhism, if she learned – really learned – the Tibetan language. Alexandra needed no further prompting.

At the invitation of the Crown Prince of Sikkim – a guest at the Dalai Lama's court and himself a considerable scholar – she travelled to Gangtok, the Sikkimese capital. The Prince placed the royal library at her disposal and assigned Dawasandup, the headmaster of the Tibetan school in Gangtok, to be her interpreter. He in turn introduced her to teachers, scholars and lamas who welcomed her interest and were happy to encourage her studies. Gradually thoughts of Paris faded from her mind, her commission from the French Ministry of Education was forgotten, and Alexandra found herself being drawn deeper and deeper into the seductive mysteries of Tibetan Buddhism. And thus her wanderings began.

*   *   *   *

Together with Dawasandup she spent several months touring Sikkim. She was introduced to religious rituals and ceremonies at remote monasteries and she studied meditation and sacred literature under a refugee Tibetan doctor of philosophy in his *gompa* or lamaserie on a lonely hilltop high in the mountains. 'Gradually I learned to lift the veil that hides the real Tibet and its religious world.' When she expressed a desire to travel northwards towards the Sikkim–Tibet border Dawasandup reluctantly announced that his teaching duties prevented him from going with her. He introduced her instead to one of his students, a fifteen-year-old Sikkimese boy named Yongden, and suggested she take him as her guide, interpreter and servant. Yongden would remain with Alexandra, first as her companion and eventually as her legally adopted son, for the rest of his life.

Apart from one calamitous trip down to Benares, where she almost instantly fell ill, Alexandra spent the next five years living, travelling and studying in the mountains. In 1914 her 'keen desire to experience the contemplative life according to lamaist methods' led her to spend ten months as a hermit in a cave 13 000 feet up in the Sikkimese Himalayas, an experience so richly fulfilling that the prospect of returning to the 'sorrowful world below' was almost more than she could bear. Incurably vague about dates, as if they somehow detracted from the sublimity of her experiences, Alexandra mentions only that 'summer was approaching' as she and Yongden ventured for the first time over the border into Tibet. Although she knew this was forbidden territory, she had learned enough about Lamaism to know that what she had seen so far in Sikkim and Nepal was only a pale reflection of the Lamaism that existed in Tibet; it was worth the risk.

> Up and up we went, skirting gigantic glaciers, catching occasional glimpses of crossing valleys filled by huge clouds. And then, without any transition, as we issued from the mists, the Tibetan tableland appeared before us, immense, void, resplendent under the luminous sky of Central Asia. . . . Nothing has ever dimmed in my mind the memory of my first sight of Tibet.

On that first occasion they did little more than walk a little and wonder greatly. Some months later, however, emboldened by this initial success, they ventured a second time into the Forbidden Land. This time they travelled as far as the famous monastery of Tashilunpo at Shigatse, home of the Tashi Lama, where Hélène Blavatsky had pursued her studies of the occult. Alexandra was gratified to find that her sojourn as a hermit had made her 'somewhat famous in the country'. The Tashi Lama welcomed her with great kindness and tried to persuade her to stay and continue her studies. She found him to be a learned, enlightened and liberal-minded man, and admitted to being sorely tempted. 'But I had not forseen such an offer. My luggage, notes, collection of photographic negatives (why should one think these things important?) had been left behind, some in the care of friends in Calcutta, others in my hermitage. How many things remained for me to learn, how great was the mental transformation necessary to enable me to become, a few years later, a joyful tramp in the wilds of Tibet.'

However she did stay for several days, talking with the Tashi Lama and enjoying earnest theological discussions with the monks of Tashilunpo. 'The novelty of what I saw and heard, the special psychic atmosphere of the place, enchanted me. I have seldom enjoyed such blissful hours.' When she at last dragged herself away the Tashi Lama bestowed on her the robe of a graduate lama and a diploma of 'Doctor *honori causa* of the Tashilunpo university'.

It was as they were leaving Tibet on this occasion that a postal runner carrying Charles Bell's letter caught up with her – and it was then that she made her vow to return. But she was in no hurry. She had no intention of attempting the journey to Lhasa until she was both physically and mentally prepared for it; then, and only then, when she had the best possible chance of succeeding, would she 'show what the will of a woman could achieve'.

Determined to extend her researches into other branches of Buddhism, Alexandra left the Himalayas in 1917 and travelled to Burma where she went into retreat in the Sagain hills with the Kamatangs, the contemplative monks of one of the most austere Buddhist sects. Crossing southern China she moved on to Japan where she stayed for a while at Tofoku-ji, a monastery of the Zen sect which, for centuries, had been the centre of study for the intellectual élite of the country. From there she travelled to Korea and spent several months meditating and studying with the novices at the forest monastery of Panya-an.

By now she had thrown off her European ways almost completely. She wore either the local dress or her honorary lama robes and travelled either on foot or by mule. She stressed that she was not, as yet, in disguise – the indigenous dress was simply the most appropriate for her purposes; only by adopting local habits, local dress and local food could she really come to know and understand the people. Her luggage was simple; a change of clothes, a few blankets, countless notebooks in which she recorded folk legends and detailed descriptions of religious myths and rituals, and her camera and ever-growing collection of photographs.

Every now and then she would bundle up a collection of articles and send them back to France where Philippe arranged for them to be published. Her earnings from these, generously supplemented from Philippe's own pocket, provided her with sufficient income to continue her travels. In 1918 she reached Peking where she had planned to stay for a while. But after a year's absence Tibet was calling her again.

For years I have dreamed of far-away Kumbum without having dared hope I would ever get there. Yet now the journey is decided. I will cross the whole of China to reach its north-western frontier into Tibetan land.

Alexandra was now fifty years old. Yet so immersed was she in her studies, and so enamoured of her solitary wandering existence, that she could face the prospect of crossing the breadth of China without a qualm. From Peking she and Yongden joined a caravan consisting of two rich lamas and their respective retinues who were returning to Tibet, a Chinese merchant and his servants, and an assortment of monks and laymen who were glad to benefit from the protection that numbers ensured on the unsafe roads. It took them seven months to cover the 2000 miles to Kumbum. In the wake of the Chinese revolution of 1911 against the Manchu dynasty, law and order had broken down and civil war was still raging through the interior. They had several times to make wide detours to avoid being plunged into fierce fighting, on more than one occasion they came under fire; and they only managed to escape from the beseiged city of Tungchow by hiding in a cart full of straw and making a dash for it during a thunderstorm. One of the most vivid images that would remain with Alexandra in later years was of a tea-party with the governor of Shensi.

> The enemy surrounds the city. Tea is served by soldiers with guns on their shoulders and revolvers in their belts, ready to resist an attack that may occur at any minute. Yet the conversation round the tea table is that of literati enjoying an intellectual game. How wonderfully refined and civilised are the Chinese and how lovable, in spite of their faults.

*   *   *   *

The Tibetan word for monastery, *gompa*, literally translates as 'house in the solitude'. The famous Kumbum *gompa*, however, was more than just a house, it was a community of some four thousand souls situated in the solitude of the ill-defined no-man's land between China and Tibet. The stone dwellings of the lamas of Kumbum clustered round the base of the hill like so many tumbled boulders and were stacked up its steep slopes as if jostling for position near the gold-domed temples that seemed to sprout from the very fabric of the rocky summit.

As a *trapa*, or student lama, Yongden was a welcome visitor to Kumbum. He and Alexandra were allocated modest living quarters in the palace precincts of the Pegyai Lama, a venerable teacher and member of the *Kagyudpas*, the 'Red Cap' sect in whose monastery Yongden had served his novitiate. Alexandra's Tibetan was now faultless, her Pali (the sacred language of Buddhism) very nearly so, and she had learned several of the regional dialects; with this knowledge even the most obscure Buddhist books and manuscripts were accessible to her. The monastery's considerable library was at their disposal, authorities on every aspect of Lamaism were their near neighbours, ceremonies and rituals, initiations and festivals were taking place daily just outside their door, and colleges for the study of philosophy, metaphysics, ritual and magic and the Sacred Scriptures were integral parts of the monastery: Kumbum was the ideal place for Alexandra to continue her studies. Still apparently in no hurry to fulfil her vow to go to Lhasa, she stayed at Kumbum for three years.

Sitting at the feet of gaunt, long-haired ascetics she learned about the mystic contemplations that would lead to spiritual enlightenment. She studied, with 'scientific interest', such psychic phenomena as *Lung-gom*, the art of covering enormous distances on foot at supernormal speeds, something like the progress made by fairytale giants in seven-league boots, and *Thumo Reskiang*, whereby the initiate learns to generate sufficient internal warmth to allow him to survive temperatures of many degrees below freezing while wrapped only in a cotton sheet, or – if expert – completely naked, for months at a time. She watched spirit mediums go into trances and speak with tongues, she was taught the efficacy of a bewildering variety of protective charms against the power of evil demons, and she encountered adepts at 'sending messages on the wind'; 'telepathy', she observed, 'is a branch of the Tibetan secret lore that seems to play the part that wireless telegraphy has recently taken in the West.'

To the uninitiated Alexandra is the ideal interpreter of 'Tibetan secret lore'. Her mind was completely open to new and strange ideas, yet she never suspended her critical faculties; she was totally absorbed in her studies, yet she never got carried away. If she could see any plausible explanation for the phenomena she witnessed, she would present this alongside the mystical version and leave the reader to decide; if, as quite often happened, she encountered frauds, she would expose them with wry humour, but she would rarely condemn; and she never tried to enhance her own reputation by being unnecessarily cryptic.

Although she shied away from the darker side of Tibetan occultism – 'the lugubrious musing and practices in which corpses play a prominent part' – she was not averse to trying her hand at a few small 'miracles' herself. These consisted mainly of prophesies based on a combination of commonsense, astute guesswork and a measure of good luck, and some simple medical cures. But she was honest enough to admit that 'chance, the faith, and the robust consitution of those who were benefited made it difficult to abstain from working wonders, and I had some gratifying success as an oracle.' In later years she would have cause to regret this gentle boast. Her reputation as a mystic led to her being assailed with demands to perform an amazing variety of miracles, ranging from requests for her to tell fortunes through pleas for help in passing exams to demands that she should cause someone to drop dead from a distance. To lighten the inevitable disappointment that followed her refusal to comply, she would explain:

> Tibetans do not believe in *miracles*, that is to say in *supernatural* happenings. They consider the extraordinary facts which astonish us to be the work of *natural* energies which come into action in special circumstances, or through the skill of someone who knows how to release them, or, sometimes, through the agency of an individual who unknowingly contains within himself the elements apt to move certain material or mental mechanisms which produce extraordinary phenomena. They believe that by a very strong and very continuous concentration of thought one can actually create the living and acting external reality of the form upon which the mental concentration is exercised. In all cases it is a matter of natural energies whose action is either spontaneous or controlled by individuals who have the capacity to do so.

She would further elucidate the nature and foundation of these beliefs by linking them to the conditions in Tibet which were peculiarly favourable for psychic phenomena; the high altitude, the great silence, the solitude, and the natural placidity of the Tibetan mind. So rational an explanation makes the sceptics who denounced her as a fraud – and there were a few – appear wrongheaded themselves.

Anyway, she would continue rather more tetchily, she had not gone to Tibet with the idea of studying miracles. She was merely 'researching the forms which Buddhism assumed in becoming Lamaism, that is to say in annexing and blending a number of doctrines and ritualistic elements borrowed from Nepalese Tantricism and from Bön, the ancient religion which dominated Tibet before the introduction of Buddhism.' All of which, according to Eric Teichman, one of the 'devious British political officers' that Alexandra so resented, comes to much the same thing. 'Had the lamas of Tibet elected to adopt Christianity instead of Buddhism in the seventh century they would probably have overlaid it with the same mass of superstition, taken from the old nature worship of the country [Bön] with which they have overlaid Buddhism.'

Her sojourn at Kumbum strongly reinforced Alexandra's own adherence to Buddhism. To an apostate Catholic the greatest glory of Buddhism was the complete spiritual freedom it granted not just to the layman but to the monks themselves. 'Each monk', she wrote euphorically, 'may believe whatever doctrine he deems true, he may even be an utter unbeliever, this concerns himself only.' And the longer she stayed in 'these majestic wilds at the summit of our globe' the better she understood and appreciated the evolution of Lamaism. Over the centuries it had become, par excellence, a religion which provided the inhabitants of one of the highest and harshest countries in the world with the spiritual means of survival in what would otherwise be grim, sometimes even intolerable conditions. 'He who knows how to go about it could live comfortably even in Hell', was a fundamental dictum in the colleges of Kumbum. At the end of three years Alexandra believed that she 'knew how to go about it'; she was ready to fulfil her vow.

★　　　★　　　★　　　★

Alexandra and Yongden left Kumbum at the end of 1922. 'Farewell! . . . Farewell! . . . We are off!', are the opening words of *My Journey to Lhasa*, setting what she thought was the appropriate tone for a travelogue. As a tribute to her by now profound knowledge of their religion and its ancient scriptures, the lamas of Kumbum conferred upon her the honorary title of lama – an honour granted to no other western woman either before or since, and one of which she remained justly proud to the end of her life.

But they had a long way to go before the real journey began. From Kumbum they travelled south for seven months through the Szechuan province of western China. At the small town of Lichiang on the Yangtse river in Yunnan they made their final preparations for the Great Adventure. Their chosen route would take them from Lichiang in a north-westerly direction round the top of Burma, across the Mekong and Salween rivers and then due west to Lhasa. By entering Tibet from China Alexandra hoped to avoid bumping into any more 'devious British political officers', and although the route was a roundabout one, it was one that few people would expect a foreigner to take. Their path would twist and climb over passes more than 18 000 feet above sea level, plummet into abysmal valleys, lose itself on grey gale-swept glaciers and meander across deserts peopled only by marauding bands of robbers. As the crow flies the distance between Lichiang and Lhasa was some 700 miles. As the pilgrim walks, however, it would be more than 1000 miles over some of the most formidable terrain on earth. And it was as pilgrims that they had decided to travel.

> Previous experience had proved to me that I could escape notice in the disguise of a poor traveller. Most of my fellow-travellers would probably be pilgrims from various regions of Tibet and my best plan was to merge into their number like a common *arjopa*. The *arjopas* are those mendicant pilgrims who, all through the year, ramble in their thousands across Tibet, going from one to another of its sacred places. The *arjopa*, not necessarily but for the most part, belongs to the religious order, either as a monk or a nun. Yongden, who is an authentic and well-read lama, looked his part perfectly, and I would travel as his aged mother undertaking a long pilgrimage for devotional reasons, thus constituting a touching and sympathetic figure.

There was a second reason for this decision. Yongden, a Sikkimese, would have no trouble in passing for a Tibetan, and as a lama no one would think to question his right to travel through Tibet. Alexandra on the other hand, despite her fluency in the language and her expertise in all things Tibetan, was still faced with an almost insuperable disadvantage. Photographs taken of her during her stay at Kumbum when she was fifty-two years old show a short, sturdy lady with a round face and an ample bosom – one would guess her to be a suburban schoolmistress maybe, or *patronne* of a Parisian café-bar. But, even in her lama's dress and pointed Tibetan hat, she did not look remotely like a Tibetan. The ragged clothes, layers of ingrained dirt and humble, self-effacing demeanor of the impoverished *arjopa* would provide her with perfect camouflage. She accordingly donned a capacious brown pilgrim robe, like an oversized belted dressing-gown, and disguised the whiteness of her skin under several layers of grime. She rubbed a stick of Chinese ink into her hair to turn it black, attached long pigtails of yak's hair, surmounted the whole with an old red belt wound into a turban and darkened her face with a mixture of cocoa and crushed charcoal.

Their possessions too had to be appropriately sparse. Alexandra parcelled up her notebooks, all their spare clothes and any such giveaway items as pens and toothbrushes and sent them to a missionary acquaintance for safe-keeping. When they found that even the meagre luggage that remained was still too heavy they discarded their blankets and waterproof groundsheet. Now they were left with the clothes they stood up in, a bowl each to eat from, an aluminium pot which was 'kettle, teapot and saucepan all in one', one long knife and two pairs of chopsticks. 'Pilgrims travelling on foot, as we pretended to be, have no more.'

She knew that nothing short of total commitment would suffice if she was to have any chance of reaching her goal. A small cotton tent to protect them from the worst of the weather, an ancient revolver and a few gold coins tucked into a money belt under her robes, and a sketch map of the route to Lhasa hidden in her boots were the only concessions she made to her true identity. But there was more to her commitment than plain commonsense. Having taken the decision to interrupt her studies in order to make this defiant gesture, she was determined to make the most of it; the journey to Lhasa had become a way not just of proving her expertise to the authorities, but of proving it to herself. Indeed, as she shouldered her small pack and prepared to take to the road, it seemed as if this journey was the natural climax to the last twelve years. The long months of study and meditation, the solitude and the self-denial and the privation seemed to have been a preparation for this supreme experience.

As they approached the Chinese–Tibetan border they left the main pilgrim road and took to small hill-paths. The Chinese and the Tibetans were just as determined as the British to keep foreigners out of Tibet, and officials of both governments would have a wary eye for any suspicious characters approaching or attempting to cross that border. The merest hint that the young lama and his elderly mother were anything other than genuine pilgrims would result in their immediate arrest. For two weeks they travelled only at night, skirting villages and often losing their way in the darkness. By day they holed up in caves or hid in the forest. They dared not pitch the tent for fear of attracting the attention of shepherds or woodcutters who might be using these same hill-paths. Instead they used it as an extra blanket, lying down in a suitable ditch or hollow with their luggage between them, and spreading the tent over the top; 'when snow had fallen that white tent spread on the ground with a few dry leaves and twigs strewn on it looked absolutely like a patch of snow amongst other patches and we felt quite safe under it.'

The discipline of Alexandra's adopted religion seems to have deserted her under the strain of these early days on the road. Far from resigning herself to whatever fate had in store, she lived in a constant state of anxiety. She forced poor Yongden to march sometimes for eighteen hours on end, refusing to let him light fires for his beloved tea and driving both him and herself to the edge of starvation and exhaustion in her determination to cross the frontier undetected. Until they were safely inside Tibet and had put some distance between themselves and the border, people of any description were to be avoided at all costs.

But if the prospect of encountering human obstacles gave her sleepless nights, physical obstacles held no fear for her. When the Lazarist priest, Father Huc, had been escorted out of Tibet through this region seventy-five years earlier he had confessed to 'breaking out in a cold sweat' at the sight of the precipitous terrain over which he was expected to travel. In *Travels in Tartary, Tibet and China, 1844–6*, published in 1851, he described how:

> From Lhasa to the Chinese border, along the whole of that great distance, there are continuous vast chains of mountains, divided by cataracts, deep ravines and narrow defiles. Sometimes these mountains are piled and jumbled together in the most monstrous shapes; at others they follow one another in a regular chain like the teeth of an immense saw. . . . Yet to the people of Tibet only those which 'claim travellers' lives' can really be called mountains. Anything that does not go soaring up into the clouds is to them a 'plain' and anything which is not a precipice or a labyrinth is a 'smooth road'.

Totally lacking from Alexandra's book would be those little descriptions and details that would have made the land and its people come to life for her readers. The average Tibetan, his home, his family, his means of making a livelihood, his landscape – all were so familiar to her that it never occurred to her to describe them for the benefit of others. Only when she was confronted by scenery, individuals or situations that were exceptional, and therefore new even to her, would she really let fly with her pen; but the 'precipitous terrain' that Huc found so monstrous did not seem to her in any way remarkable. In this respect, as in so many others, Alexandra was more Tibetan than European; the mountains were worthy of her attention not for their physical proportions but for their individual auras; her response to each one depended not on its height or the steepness of its slopes, but on its character. Some were benign, soothing, even inviting. Others had to be approached with humility or reverence. Some, and not always the highest, had to be avoided altogether.

Towering in a clear sky lit by a full moon, the mountains on either side of the 18 000-foot Dokar Pass did not appear to her as 'the menacing guardians of an impassable frontier' but looked more like 'worshipful but affable Deities standing at the threshold of a mystic land, ready to welcome and protect the adventurous lover of Tibet'. Sure enough, they crossed the frontier without further incident and then travelled for a week along the high paths without meeting another soul. Finally they decided that the time had come for them to join the pilgrims' way.

*   *   *   *

The 'roads' in this part of Tibet were in reality a network of tracks leading from village to village. Sometimes these paths were little more than steep, barely discernible goat-tracks; but where several paths converged they might open out for a while into a well-trodden highway wide enough to allow two or three riders to travel abreast. Few others would be making exactly the same journey or travelling at the same speed as Alexandra and Yongden. Although they might fall in with one group or another for a few days, sooner or later their paths would diverge again as they headed off in different directions. This suited Alexandra perfectly. Too long an association with any one group would greatly increase the chance of her making a slip that would lead to her discovery. Their fellow-travellers too, most of whom were pilgrims, came from a wide variety of Tibetan regions; they wore different clothes, spoke different dialects and varied widely in appearance. Alexandra and Yongden hoped to merge into the motley crowd, their own peculiarities of appearance, dress or accent unremarkable amongst such diversity. A pilgrim from the north of the country who asked them where they came from could be told that they came from the south, and vice versa. Too persistent an enquirer could be dropped a casual hint that the lama was a *nagspa*, a sorcerer, or that his mother was a *pamo*, a female medium possessed by gods or demons – Alexandra would illustrate this with an awesome grimace or a cackling laugh or pretend to fall into a trance, and the terrified inquisitor would take to his heels.

The fact that Yongden was a lama made their lives very much easier. The local villagers, on whose sympathy and generosity they relied, believed that they would gain spiritual merit by giving alms and assistance to a holy man and it salved Alexandra's conscience to know that there were certain services a lama was expected to provide in return for such alms. At every village the sight of the lama striding round the corner brought the inhabitants scuttling out of their homes. In a trice Yongden would be surrounded by supplicants begging him to reveal to them the whereabouts of a lost cow, or to recite prayers for the soul of a recently deceased relative.

Few of these villagers paid any attention to the little brown-robed lady, leaning on her pilgrim staff, eyes cast humbly to the ground, who followed in his wake. Yongden would intone the appropriate prayers or cast stones into the air to study the pattern of their fall. Alexandra, meanwhile, would quietly set about gathering fuel for their fire and water for their tea, secure in the knowledge that Yongden's eloquence would earn them a handful of barley flour or a few dried apricots for the meal.

Vague as ever about dates, Alexandra mentions only that they started out from Lichiang in the autumn of 1923 and travelled through the winter. The altitude of the Tibetan plateau and its position in the centre of a vast continent mean that the air is dry. Snowfall is restricted to the higher ranges, leaving the valleys clear and passable throughout all but the severest winters. But the cold is intense, bitter winds blowing down from the icy tops penetrate even the thickest of sheltering forests and severe night frosts freeze the lakes and rivers.

There were long stretches of every path that passed through no habitation at all, and over the higher ranges the traveller faced the prospect of days at a time with no forests for shelter, no villages for hospitality and precious little fuel to make a fire. No pilgrim in his right mind would refuse such luxuries where they were still on offer. Were Alexandra and Yongden to arrive in the vicinity of a village and then insist on retiring into the forest or to a cave to camp alone, as was their true preference, they would immediately become objects of intense curiosity and even suspicion. In order to sustain their disguise they therefore had to accept any hospitality that came their way.

In even the poorest household Yongden, as a lama, could be sure of the tastiest morsel from the communal pot and a sheepskin rug on the patch of floor nearest the fire to sleep on. Alexandra, on the other hand, was considered of little importance, and dared not assert herself in any way. She had to be content with a seat on the rough and dirty floor in a far corner, the poorest dregs of what was usually a fairly unappetising meal to eat, and, if she was lucky, a small square of sacking as a mattress. But she was more than ready to appreciate the compensations. 'I knew that such penance would not be without reward. I was living near the very soul and heart of the masses of that unknown land, near those of its womenfolk whom no outsider had ever encountered.' Just occasionally, though, she would sigh for the times when their roles had been reversed.

> Years before, when we travelled in the northern country and I wore my beautiful lama robes, it was I who was requested to bless the people, blow on the sick to cure them, and prophesy about countless things. That glorious time was gone. Now I humbly washed our pot in the stream while Yongden solemnly revealed to his attentive listeners the secrets of the future.

Alexandra's relationship with Yongden was touching in its mutual devotion. This strong, solitary, single-minded woman, so fiercely jealous of her independence and her freedom, lavished on the young Sikkimese boy all the affection and emotion that seemed to be lacking in any of her other relationships. She taught him to speak French and English, she shared her studies, her possessions and her thoughts with him, and her pride in his achievements and the strength of her feelings of responsibility for his welfare could not have been greater had he indeed been her natural son.

Yongden, for his part, was more loyal and more devoted to Alexandra than most mothers dare to hope their sons will ever be. He seems to have accepted her tyranny and her affection with equal composure; now twenty-five years old, he had been with her for ten years without a break, he endured danger and discomfort and even risked death at her side or for her sake, and he acted as her companion, secretary, servant, adviser, whipping boy or hero depending on her whim of the moment with – if Alexandra is to be believed – never a word of complaint.

*   *   *   *

As they approached the most forbidding of the ranges that lay across their path Alexandra lets slip that it was now December. They had thus been walking for more than two months. Although she still lived in daily expectation of being unmasked, she could not help being proud of the expertise with which she was handling her role. She could wail as pitifully as the most destitute of beggars, she could pray as long and loud as the holiest of pilgrims, and most satisfactory of all, she had learned to live and even thrive on the most frugal of diets.

She attributed her excellent health to 'pure air, long tramps', and her insistence, whatever the circumstances, on starting every day with a hot cup of salted tea. When hunger did strike she would remind herself sternly that she had not come to Tibet 'to indulge in gastronomy' and concentrate instead on making the most of the delicacies that did come their way – a turnip, a radish, or a small piece of dried bacon. These titbits would be boiled up into a watery soup to accompany the *tsampa*, barley flour kneaded into a thick dough with tea, water, or butter, that was their staple food. One meal a day was their ration.

Faced, though, with the prospect of climbing to an altitude of something over 17 000 feet to cross the next pass, Alexandra waived this strict rule and decided to make a particularly good breakfast of both soup and tea. Thus refreshed she 'looked boldly to the range silhouetted against the horizon and felt capable of climbing to the sky'. With a flourish of Gallic rhetoric she would recall:

> How happy I was to be there, en route for the mystery of these unexplored heights, alone, in the great silence, tasting the sweets of solitude and tranquility.

It soon transpired that they had seriously underestimated the 'mystery of the unexplored heights'. The sketch maps that Alexandra had carefully hidden in her boots were useless. She had already discovered that the names on them in no way corresponded to the names used by the inhabitants and that the rivers and mountains were never in the right places. But knowing that it would have been out of character for pilgrims to display curiosity about what lay ahead, they had been able to make only the vaguest and most general enquiries about the route across the mountains. There had been talk of a hamlet, of yak herds, and even of a notable shrine in the valley on the far side – and that had been enough. Now, as they struggled upwards, Alexandra found herself regretting her reticence. The horizon ahead seemed to stay as remote as ever, however far they climbed, and with every added metre of altitude the air grew colder and the icy wind more piercing.

At last they reached the pass, which Alexandra reckoned to be at about 19 000 feet. Instead of looking down into the next sheltered and possibly hospitable valley, they found themselves staring out over a vast, undulating, snow-covered plateau, ringed, apparently on all sides, by towering frozen summits. There was no sign of a track and no indication of which way they should go.

> The disproportion between the giant glacier range, that wild and endless slope, and the two puny travellers who had ventured alone in that extraordinarily phantasmagoric land of the heights, impressed me as it had never done before. An inexpressible feeling of compassion moved me to the bottom of my heart. It could not be possible that my young friend, the companion of so many of my adventurous travels, should meet his end on that mountain. I would find the way; it was my duty. I knew that I would.

And of course somehow she did. For eight days they climbed, scrambled and floundered through deep snow, over passes, down steep-sided valleys and across bleak, wind-scoured plains. They finished all their food and existed for three days on a diet of melted snow. When there was no fuel to be found Alexandra decided to practise the *thumo* rites she had learned at Kumbum. Sitting on the ground with the flint and a piece of moss under her clothes, she went into the required trance. Within a few minutes she 'felt fire bursting out of my head and of my fingers' and before long a little heap of grass and dried cow dung was flickering into life-saving flames.

Her relation of episodes like this was, inevitably, fodder to those sceptics who doubted whether she had ever been to Lhasa. How could anyone believe such mumbo-jumbo nonsense? To such criticism Alexandra would only reply that she did not care whether or not anyone believed in such phenomena and had no desire to convince them. Whether the heat she generated was real or imaginary was irrelevant – all that was certain was that the exercise of mystic powers had enabled her, on more than one occasion, to survive under conditions that would otherwise have been intolerable.

Certainly the strains and tensions of the journey and the months of punishing effort at consistently high altitude were having a dramatic effect on her mental as well as her physical state. The wizened, weather-beaten little figure tramping resolutely across the Tibetan heights was now spider-thin. The effects of hunger and fatigue were intensifying her tendency to seek out and then abandon herself to the mystical element in every experience. Lack of proper nourishment and the rarity of the atmosphere had brought her to a level of heightened awareness bordering on the halucinatory.

When there was no sign, even at the end of a week, of human habitation, of yak herds or of the famous shrine she felt no anxiety, only an exhilarating sense of solitude, 'as if we were the first inhabitants and masters of the earth'. Snow started falling so heavily that it threatened to bury them, but she noticed only that the size of the flakes made them look like beautiful butterflies. When they had to walk all through the night to keep warm because there was no hope of lighting a fire, even with the help of *thumo*, in such a blizzard, she just shook her bony fist at the elements and laughed at her struggles. No sooner had the blizzard abated and the sky cleared, at last showing them the way down off this seemingly boundless white plain, than Yongden slipped and fell into a shallow crevasse, severely spraining his ankle. Alexandra airily announced that she would carry him down the mountain. But the feat turned out to be beyond even her.

In spite of my goodwill and strenuous efforts, I was soon compelled to realise that I lacked the strength necessary to carry him across deep snow, with stones and pits hidden under it which made me stumble frequently. Yongden, who had reluctantly obeyed my express command to let himself be carried, then endeavoured to proceed leaning on me and on his staff, creeping rather than walking and stopping every ten minutes.

By the time they reached the shelter of the first trees they had seen in more than a week Yongden was barely conscious and Alexandra's boots had worn out. One more night without a fire or any hot food would almost certainly have killed them. Mercifully, just as darkness was falling, they sighted a hamlet. When they knocked on the door of the first house the owner gazed in amazement. Where had they come from? The passes had been closed by snow for days – it was really a wonder; they must be holy indeed to have achieved such a miracle. In the land that Alexandra had been led to believe was peopled by brigands and thieves, they suddenly found every door open to them and every householder anxious to gain merit by entertaining two such venerable beings.

Although they were still 300 miles from Lhasa, Alexandra felt that their successful crossing of the heights was a good omen. The route was now easy and the countryside unexpectedly beautiful. Needless to say she did not elaborate, but Eric Teichman, who had spent two years marching backwards and forwards across Eastern Tibet engaged in what would now be called shuttle-diplomacy between the Chinese and the Tibetans, was more forthcoming. He described the region as 'a country of snow peaks, rolling grassland, deep narrow valleys, pine forests and rushing torrents, resembling in some parts Switzerland, in others the downs of England and the moors of Scotland, and in others the pine-clad valleys of British Columbia'. Yongden warned Alexandra against undue optimism, but her spirits would not be suppressed. Ignoring her companion's advice she chatted freely to pilgrim and villager alike, she took detours off the path to explore tempting byways, and felt brave enough to venture the odd prophecy, benediction or even curse when the moment arose. One surly housewife, who refused them accommodation on the excuse (phoney, Alexandra thought) that she had a sick relative in the house, was startled to see the lama's old crone of a mother execute a graphic pantomime outside her window which ended with a vigorous shaking of the skirts of her robe 'as if to liberate a host of devils who had been sheltering in it'. Repenting instantly of her inhospitality, the terrified woman begged Alexandra and Yongden to spend the night in her house, but Alexandra turned and walked away with her nose in the air. An embarrassed Yongden had time to lift the curse with a quick blessing before hurrying down the road after his jubilant 'mother'.

The one remaining barrier that lay between them and Lhasa was the toll station at Giamda, a sizeable garrison and market town on an upper tributary of the Brahmaputra river. Here they would have to appear before an official in order to get a pass to proceed to the capital and they spent several sleepless nights trying to work out a strategy for getting through undetected. They need not have worried. Giamda was thronged with pilgrims from all over Tibet heading for Lhasa in time for the New Year festival; one more lama and one more old lady would be entirely unremarkable in such a crowd. They crossed the bridge, paid the toll and were issued with their pass without the official giving them a second glance.

Now it was Yongden's turn to feel relaxed and carefree and to enjoy the fellowship of the road. But Alexandra was unaware of the scenery, oblivious to the cold and indifferent to the company. Her eyes fixed on the horizon, she walked like one in a trance, every nerve tingling. Once again she gives no dates, but as the Tibetan New Year almost always falls in February, this meant that they had been walking for four months. At last the end was in sight.

Alexandra was convinced that their entrance into Lhasa was attended by a miracle. No sooner had they caught their first glimpse of the towering edifice of the mighty Potala palace, 'capped with golden roofs, uplifted high in the blue sky on a shining pedestal of dazzling white buildings', than the whole scene was obliterated by a violent dust storm. Not just Alexandra and Yongden but every man, woman and child in the streets was forced to cover their face to avoid being suffocated by the dense, whirling cloud of sand. It would have been impossible to recognise your own mother in such circumstances, let alone identify one out of a stream of newly-arrived pilgrims. No one suspected that 'for the first time in history a foreign woman was entering the Forbidden City'.

The storm abated as suddenly as it had arisen. Bewildered by the noise and the crowds after months spent in the solitudes, and perhaps still more bewildered by their good fortune, Alexandra and Yongden found themselves standing in the middle of Lhasa in a daze, with no idea what to do or where to go. Unexpected help came in the shape of a young woman moved to compassion by Alexandra's gaunt appearance. She led them to a 'ramshackle cottage' occupied by beggars where they were given the use of a narrow cell. It was perfect – nobody would ever think of looking for a foreigner in such an unsavoury corner of the city. Even the cautious Yongden was forced to admit that at last they had succeeded – they were in Lhasa.

Almost before he had had time to draw breath, the young lama found himself being whirled around the sights of the city by his triumphant 'mother'.

All things which are Lhasa's own beauty and peculiarity would have to be seen by the lone woman explorer who had had the nerve to come to them from afar, the first of her sex. It was my well-won reward after the trials of the road and the vexations by which for several years various officials had endeavoured to prevent my wanderings in Tibet. This time I intended that nobody should deprive me of it.

First, and most important of all, they made a tour of the Potala palace, where a yellow-robed lama made Alexandra's heart miss a beat by telling her to remove her bonnet. Luckily in the gloom of the narrow passages illuminated only by flickering butter lamps, no one noticed anything strange. They explored bazaars and visited shrines. They followed religious processions through the steep, twisting streets and joined the crowds of pilgrims in a tour of the lamaseries to celebrate the New Year.

The final festival was to be attended by no less a person than the thirteenth Dalai Lama, who had returned to Tibet from exile in 1913. Alexandra could not help wondering what he would have said had he known that among the clamouring, milling throng surrounding his parade through the streets of Lhasa was the very same French woman to whom he had granted an audience twelve years before. But she was not tempted to reveal herself – even the omnipotence of His Supreme Holiness would be unlikely to save her from instant expulsion. Rather she preferred to run, push, laugh and shout with the crowd, 'enjoying, as a youngster might have done, the fun of being in Lhasa for the New Year'. She found herself being shoved in the back by 'giants in sheepskins', jostled by drunken revellers and finally hit by a policeman with a truncheon for straying into the path of a passing nobleman.

> Truly I had to make a great effort to prevent myself from giving him a tip, so delighted was I with the fun. 'What a wonderful incognito is mine', I confided to Yongden. 'Now I am even beaten in the street'. After that I felt completely secure.

★　　　★　　　★　　　★

They stayed in Lhasa for two months. But when rumours started to circulate that a foreigner had been seen in the city, Alexandra knew that it was time to go. She claimed still to be in rude health, but privately acknowledged that she was little more than skin and bone. If she was to have the strength to make the journey home she had better leave now.

> So, one sunny morning in spring, I followed once more the wide street that led out of the city, leaving Lhasa as quietly as I had entered. We crossed the river and ascended a small pass. I looked back for one last time and then, turning to the south, began my descent. Lhasa had gone forever from my eyes and taken its place in my world of memories.

Her homeward journey was in marked contrast to the outward one. Although she still travelled in disguise, Alexandra knew that official surveillance of travellers heading away from Lhasa would be far less strict than of those heading towards it. It was no longer quite so crucial to be inconspicuous – after all, the worst that could happen to her if she was discovered was that she would be thrown out and she was leaving anyway. She had therefore allowed herself the luxury of a bath and a new set of clothes and left Lhasa dressed as what she called a 'lower-middle-class woman'. She had acquired a servant and two horses, one to ride and one to carry her possessions which had been considerably increased by her purchase in Lhasa of a quantity of books to add to the already substantial library she had collected on her previous journeys.

'I felt very tempted to turn eastwards', she wrote, 'and reach Yunnan by a new route.' But she had something more important to do. So she took instead the road south to Sikkim and, in the middle of August 1924, she arrived on the doorstep of the British Trade Agent in Gyantse. David MacDonald was 'dumbfounded'. At her request he signed a statement testifying to her arrival in Gyantse on her way from Eastern Tibet through Lhasa. Alexandra had made her point.

*   *   *   *

Having reached the end of her 'diversion' Alexandra picked up the threads of her scholastic life. In 1925 she returned to France to write her book, taking Yongden with her. Her journey, and the book, made her a celebrity. She was awarded the Gold Medal of the Geographical Society of France and made a Chevalier of the Légion d'Honneur. For ten years she made her home in a small cottage in the French Alps, writing copiously on her travels and on every aspect of Tibetan Buddhism, and cataloguing, with Yongden's help, her extensive library of books and manuscripts.

In 1936, when she was sixty-eight years old, she returned to Central Asia. Always with Yongden by her side, she spent the six years of the Second World War living at Tachienlu on Tibet's eastern border, still writing, studying and travelling through her beloved mountains. Not until she was seventy-six years old did she finally retire to her home in France. Yongden, her adopted son, died in Digne in 1955 at the age of fifty-five. Alexandra herself lived on until 1969 when she died just a few weeks before her one hundred and first birthday.

BIBLIOGRAPHY

EMILY EDEN

BARR, P. and DESMOND, R. *Simla: hill station in British India* Scolar Press, 1977.

DUNBAR, J. *Golden Interlude: the Edens in India 1836–42* J. Murray, 1955.op.

EDEN, E. *Letters from India* London, 1872.op.

EDEN, E. *Miss Eden's letters* Ed. V. Dickinson. Macmillan, 1919.op.

EDEN, E. *Portraits of the Princes and People of India* London, 1844.op.

EDEN, E. *Up the country* Virago, 1983.

EDEN, F. *Tigers, Durbars and Kings: Indian journals, 1837–38* Ed. J. Dunbar. J. Murray, 1988.

TROTTER, L. *The Earl of Auckland* IN *Rulers of India* Ed. W.W. Hunter. Clarendon Press, 1980.op.

ANNA LEONOWENS

BOCK, C. *Temples and Elephants: travels in Siam in 1881–82* O.U.P., 1986.

BRISTOWE, W.S. *Louis and the King of Siam* Chatto & Windus, 1976.op.

HALL, D.G.E. *History of South-east Asia* Macmillan, 1981.op.

LANDON, M.D. *Anna and the King of Siam* H. Hamilton, 1956.op.

LEONOWENS, A. *English Governess at the Siamese Court* A. Barker, London, 1954.op.

LEONOWENS, A. *Life and Travels in India* Porter & Coates, 1884.op.

LEONOWENS, A. *Romance of the Harem* Boston, 1873.op.

LEONOWENS, A. *Siamese Harem Life* A. Barker, 1952.op.

MOFFAT, A.L. *Mongkut, King of Siam* Cornell University Press, 1961.op.

AMELIA EDWARDS

EDWARDS, A. *A Thousand Miles up the Nile* Century, 1982.

EDWARDS, A. *Untrodden Peaks and Unfrequented Valleys: midsummer ramble in the Dolomites* Virago, 1986.

FAGAN, B.M. *The Rape of the Nile: tomb robbers, tourists and archaeologists in Egypt* Macdonald & Jane's, 1977.op.

LITTLE, T. *High Dam at Aswan: the subjugation of the Nile* Methuen, 1965.op.

MOOREHEAD, A. *The Blue Nile* Penguin, 1983.

MOOREHEAD, A. *The White Nile* H. Hamilton, 1960; Penguin, 1963, 1971,op; 1973.

KATE MARSDEN

ALLEN, A. *Travelling Ladies* Jupiter, 1981.op.

JOHNSON, H. *Life of Kate Marsden* Simpkin, Marshall & Co., 1895.op.

MARSDEN, K. *By Sledge and Horseback to Outcast Siberian Lepers* Century, 1986.

MIDDLETON, D. *Victorian Lady Travellers* Routledge & Kegan Paul, 1965.op.

SEMENOV, Y. *Siberia: its conquest and development* Trans. J.R. Foster. Hollis & Carter, 1963.op.

WEYMOUTH, A. *Through the Leper Squint* Selwyn & Blount, 1938.op.

GERTRUDE BELL

BELL, G.L. *Amurath to Amurath* Macmillan, 1924.op.

BELL, G.L. *Letters* Ed. Lady Florence Bell. Penguin, 1987.

BELL, G.L. *Safar nameh. Persian pictures. A book of travel* J. Cape, 1937.op.

BELL, G.L. *The Desert and The Sown* Virago, 1985; Darf Publications, 1985.

BELL, G.L. and RAMSAY, W. *The thousand and one Churches* Hodder & Stoughton, 1909.op.

BURGOYNE, E. *Gertrude Bell: from her personal papers* 2 vols. Benn, 1961.op.

DOUGHTY, C. *Travels in Arabia Deserta* Dover Publications, 1980.

GLENDINNING, V. *Vita: life of V. Sackville-West* Weidenfeld & Nicholson, 1983; Penguin, 1984.

MANSFIELD, P. *The Arabs* Penguin, 1985.

PALGRAVE, W.G. *Personal narrative of a year's journey through central and eastern Arabia* Darf Publications, 1985.op.

WINSTONE, H.V.F. *Gertrude Bell* Cape, 1978; Quartet, 1980.op.

DAISY BATES

ALLEN, A. *Travelling Ladies* Jupiter, 1981.op.

BATES, D. *The Passing of the Aborigines* J. Murray, 1938.op.

BOLAM, A.G. *Trans-Australian Wonderland* Melbourne, 1930.op.

HILL, E. *Kabbarli: a personal memoir of Daisy Bates* Angus & Robertson, 1973.op.

MOORHEAD, A. *Fatal Impact: an account of the invasion of the South Pacific, 1767–1840* H. Hamilton; Penguin, 1968.op.

SALTER, E. *Daisy Bates: 'The Great White Queen of the Never-Never'* Angus & Robertson, 1972; Corgi, 1973.op.

ALEXANDRA DAVID-NEEL

CAREY, W. *Travel and Adventure in Tibet* Hodder & Stoughton, 1902.op.

DAVID-NEEL, A. *My Journey to Lhasa* Virago, 1983.

DAVID-NEEL, A. *Magic and Mystery in Tibet* Souvenir Press, 1967; Corgi, 1971; Abacus, 1977.op. Unwin, 1984.

HOPKIRK, P. *Trespassers on the Roof of the World* J. Murray, 1982; O.U.P., 1983.

HUC, R.E. *Lamas of the Western Heavens* Trans. C. de Salis. Folio Society, 1982.op.

MILLER, L. *On Top of the World: five women explorers in Tibet* Mountaineers, U.S., 1985.

TEICHMAN, E. *Travels of a Consular Officer in Eastern Tibet* C.U.P., 1922.op.

TUCCI, H.E.G. and GHERSI, E. *Secrets of Tibet* Blackie, 1935.op.